China Counting

China Counting

How the West was lost

Alex Mackinnon
and
Barnaby Powell

palgrave
macmillan

First published 2010 by
PALGRAVE MACMILLAN

Palgrave Macmillan in the UK is an imprint of Macmillan Publishers Limited, registered in England, company number 785998, of Houndmills, Basingstoke, Hampshire RG21 6XS.

Palgrave Macmillan in the US is a division of St Martin's Press LLC, 175 Fifth Avenue, New York, NY 10010.

Palgrave Macmillan is the global academic imprint of the above companies and has companies and representatives throughout the world.

Palgrave® and Macmillan® are registered trademarks in the United States, the United Kingdom, Europe and other countries.

ISBN 978–0–230–23403–1

This book is printed on paper suitable for recycling and made from fully managed and sustained forest sources. Logging, pulping and manufacturing processes are expected to conform to the environmental regulations of the country of origin.

A catalogue record for this book is available from the British Library.

A catalog record for this book is available from the Library of Congress.

10   9   8   7   6   5   4   3   2   1
19   18   17   16   15   14   13   12   11   10

Printed and bound in Great Britain by
CPI Antony Rowe, Chippenham and Eastbourne

CONTENTS

> Chinese overseas expansion is clearly accelerating. The global door is held open not only by hordes of swift feet but also by hoards of credit and cash.
>
> (Mackinnon and Powell, 2008)

In writing this book, we are conscious of the continuing flow of written material on China and its place in the world. We have therefore tried to capture a contrarian tone in this, the second of our books on China's entry to the world stage. We should in fact say re-entry or reappearance: China dominated the world several centuries ago but did not, as the denizens of Madison Avenue might put it, market itself very well. Indeed, China has until recently been most inward-looking – even to the point of imitating a hermit, a hermit with a large army, of course.

It is, however, the fall of the West that we wish to juxtapose with China's rise: the greed of Western financial houses, the selfishness of Western consumers, the lust for power of Western politicians, the military offensives in the Middle East, the hand-wringing and hand-washing over Africa – Sudan, Somalia and Zimbabwe, in particular. All these Western moral failures have allowed China as a nation, often deemed to be totalitarian in its attitude to society, to take, slowly but surely and step by step, control over the world's resources and trade.

There is nothing in our book to say how this increasing control by China can be stopped or even wrested away. This book says how to accept it, how to understand it, how to reciprocate and how to ensure that Chinese society does not make the mistakes of our own 'liberal' democracies. We are not advocating appeasement or claiming 'peace in our time' but we are pointing out that knowing China and the Chinese is the first step in a new Long March, away from economies underwritten by political lobbying, from poverty reinforced by financial chicanery, from greed tempered only by fear. In short, we argue that the West has lost the plot and it is China that really counts if we wish for an improvement in our global society. We are urging the ostrich in all of us to lift our heads from the sand and look around at what is coming our way.

We would be wrong not to acknowledge those who have gone before. The works of David Hume and Adam Smith allow us to compare the original thinking of philosophy and economics during Europe's age of enlightenment with the warped offspring that exists today. How could so many modern economists and powerful politicians have let the financial world destroy so much in so short a time?

We also acknowledge the contributions of many of our respondents who have worked and studied in China and in the West, and who have allowed us the opportunity to tap their vast knowledge into the small cup of thought this book carefully holds. We would in particular like to thank the European Chambers of Commerce in Beijing, Shanghai and Taipei. Their feedback was invaluable.

Dr Sarah Dauncey, at Sheffield University in England, and Pat Wood, Director of External Business at London Metropolitan Business School, provided opportunities and openings to test the industrial market. Professor John Bowers at Scotland's Stirling University, and Mr Wei Hua at Only College of Jiaotong University in Shanghai provided insights into the nature of joint programmes for international development.

The help and encouragement from Palgrave Macmillan, in particular Stephen Rutt and Eleanor Davey-Corrigan, were invaluable in keeping us on course. To Keith Povey and Elaine Towns for their copy-editing, we can only apologise for our tinkering. Finally, to those who offered advice we did not take, we also apologise – you will probably be right in the long run, but then, as Keynes might have said, by the time China takes over the world there may not, at this rate of erosion, be much left; and we'll be dead.

ALEX MACKINNON
BARNABY POWELL

Figure

Tables

Introduction

> To relieve the present exigency is always the object which principally interests those immediately concerned in the administration of public affairs. The future liberation of the public revenue, they leave to the care of posterity.
> (Adam Smith, *The Wealth of Nations*, Vol. II, p. 534)

In our first book *China Calling: a foot in the global door* we describe how reforms over the past centuries have shaped modern China, allowing it to open doors in global trade and finance. With Western governments frantically trying to meet the financial exigencies of today, posterity will note that China's foot is now well and truly wedged into those doors. The global credit crunch and recession of 2008 and 2009 reduced the value of Chinese investments in the West, yet paradoxically strengthened Chinese influence across the world, changing the balance of power.

Balancing that paradox highlights change in Western global authority. The *Financial Times* (the FT), a global financial newspaper and commentator, noted in the early summer of 2009 that the US authorities 'conclusively lost the boom-and-bust war'. The FT still fails to grasp the metaphorical nettle by not continuing its preliminary logic and stating that the West – the US and Europe – have thus lost the authority to wage *any* political or economic war. The Western leaders of the modern world are trapped in their precarious paradigm of liberal democracy and its 'running dogma' of capitalism. The poverty of Western political decision-making is best encapsulated by Premier Wen Jiabao, who said in March 2009 that he was 'a little worried' over the security of Chinese assets held in the USA. We pointed out in *China Calling* that an Asian 'yes' means 'maybe', and an Asian 'maybe' means 'no'. Take it as read, therefore, that 'a little' means 'a lot'.

This book aims to explain, therefore, how China's worries affect the West and how the West lost its way in the social and economic maze. China is starting to count its debtors and its dues. We get behind that inscrutability and parade the global winners and losers. In doing so, we provide a context not previously understood, an opinion that differs from most, and predict a difficult future direction for a world now dictated by Chinese decisions.

Western greed and Chinese fear

Opinion in the West tends towards China having had a free ride on the back of Western consumerism. This book attacks that opinion by demonstrating how China has in truth subsidized the West. China has watched a debt-driven spree of consumer spending infect the majority of developed countries. Western governments gained from increased collections of direct and indirect taxation; Western bankers helped investment portfolios to switch from low-interest savings into stock and housing markets; Western finance houses packaged debt into collateralized obligations (now you see it, now you don't) and Western taxpayers are now paying the bills of the bankers. China did not have a free ride – it was exhorted, constantly, to join the financial merry-go-round but its pragmatic principles held it back.

China should therefore gain from the enormous burden placed on the Western taxpayer. China has seen, quite recently, economic disaster under communist edicts of centralization. It has also felt the power of economic growth from partial capitalist decentralization. It is therefore better placed, with trillions of US dollars to spend, and with a people better prepared to weather economic recession than those in the impoverished West. But China still has cash to count.

China's sovereign funds were persuaded to enter capitalist transactions in 2006 and 2007, and its people were persuaded to follow the capitalist model. Its politicians were persuaded to follow liberal democratization, to forgo central authority and regulatory control in the name of 'human rights'. Its fear of being wrong is now tempered by a belief in one-party control with people's 'human obligations' more important than their rights. The Western taxpayer who has to pay for his or her government's banking bailout will tell you that human rights do not apply to the internal Inland Revenue services – those tax bills are obligations. Welcome to the Chinese way of doing things. As the ancient Emperor said to his taxpaying peasants – tremble and obey!

Western economic theory is thus challenged in its pervasive failure to govern markets. Chinese pragmatic theory is working and its success is global. We must not forget that it is the people on Main Street who suffer when economies go wrong, while the 'fat cats' rise above the wrath of the populace. Western democracy is touted as wonderful, but votes do not fill the belly and China cannot afford such a miserly repast. Asian poverty is much more radical. There is a mandate from below in China; the Party will make sure it continues in its national dream by serving its non-democratic people, using force if necessary, knowing that revolution is the default response to political failure.

So how will the Chinese begin to behave under the changing rules of a global game? Will the West be forced to obey, to kowtow and tug its forelock, cap in hand, asking for a bail-out? Probably. Cash is king and, as the US Treasury knows, most of it is held in the East. Asian thrift is more common than Asian profligacy. So do not expect Chinese cash to be spent in the West; China will use it for internal stability and external control. This book explains why and where.

We do so by rehearsing 'POEMS', as an acronym or mnemonic for the central issues that form the focus of this book. The political, opportunistic and environmental behaviors of the Chinese are coupled with their present might and societal habits to fix the context in Part I. Then, in Part II, we develop our opinion on how China's power base, its opportunities to modify its economic model for equilibrium in energy supply and consumption, its rising military muscle, and its improved scientific development are dependent on China's views of the West. Finally, in Part III we forecast how China's potential will lead to futuristic outcomes evolving from a masterly use of strategic global positioning. Poetical but practical!

Fixing a context

There have been many demands of an 'if only' nature made in the West. If only the Chinese had democracy, if only they had a proper taxation system, if only they had a better legal system, if only their military was not quite so strong, if only they had open government, if only they would be more like us. But they have not and are not. They behave differently. They solve problems differently. They are, in body and soul, quite different. Just how different is addressed in Part I.

There are three fixed stars to follow if Chinese behavior is to be understood. First, China is a low trust country. Second, China is not used to dealing with foreigners. Third, China is a vast nation of different tribes and dialects. Thus suspicion of anyone outside a local group or community is almost paranoid in its nature. Unlike the Western republics and monarchies, the Chinese traditionally sheltered from the Emperor's guards and spies through a strictly controlled network system. This system of connections is a protection, a defence, a bunker from the authorities, from foreigners, from the world's uncertainties, and from themselves. The Chinese will never give it up, so we must place it in its context.

Relational networks and connections control Chinese practices and behavior. In the West, unfortunately, the network concept has become confused with social connections. Chinese networks are systems, systems for exchange of knowledge and goods without internal waste but with maximum future gain. The systems, the networks, are called *guanxi*. They also call their transactional and information system *guanxi*. There is a cost associated with *guanxi*. Try uttering the word while rubbing your forefinger and thumb together – it helps to emphasize the cost of connections. Better still, think mobile phone networks: there is both a cost of using a network and a cost of linking to another.

These networks therefore generate internal trust to counter external uncertainty. Benefits are enjoyed when trust is high and costs are low within a network. To expand power and gain resources, each network increases its links to other networks – including foreigners – but this takes time and a great deal of 'getting to know you'. To maintain this link across communities and different tribes, there is a demand for future reciprocity. Within *guanxi* there is both trust and resources, but also always a future return or obligation called *renqing*.

The context is clear. Politically, do not trust the system unless you are part of it (just connect to the Party bosses); forget democracy (why vote for someone you do not know); and forget about filing taxes (just pay the fine). Practice opportunistic behavior by taking advantage of those who are not connected. Damn the environment unless it affects the personal network. Expand the military and do not respect any treaties signed under duress. China is a society tied down by its lack of trust. It will not take the lead in global affairs but will respond to positive and negative behavior – it will reciprocate in kind.

What implications for international behavior arise from such a brief introduction to the Chinese context? First, any reliance on legal controls implies that the terms should be as simple as possible (law schools, please note). Second, a long-term agreement is a short one kept open. Agreements are uncertain unless a trusting relationship of mutual reciprocity exists. Therefore, in global terms, the guardians of the cultural and mineral resources of Africa and the Middle East should prefer a Chinese relationship to a North American contract. The former suits cultural preferences for relational deals, while the latter does not.

Chinese practices and their network dynamics need to be viewed as a group control and interpreted in a holistic fashion. Unfortunately, there is no unified thinking in the West. Westerners are too individualistic. There are many alternatives open to challenge in Western formal problem solving. The Chinese, on the other hand, are practical people and seek action. The expansionary nature of China's political, economic and military governance can be explained by transacting simply for what you want, by increasing your overall resources and by keeping options open. It works.

Forming an opinion

The important Western question, however, is not how China behaves, but how that behavior affects the West. This selfish question will be answered in Part III. Explaining how the Chinese context affects China's view of the West is the purpose of Part II. If China's own ways of doing things are such that Western theory is useless, then how can we work out what China believes? Unfortunately, Chinese society makes for a distrustful and complex reading of itself, of its neighbors and of foreigners.

Traditionally, China retained its integrity by rejecting barbarian intrusion. The old imperial ways were initially challenged by Dr Sun Yat-sen and then officially swept away by external interference and internal strife. China has suffered remarkably during the twentieth century and into the twenty-first. The movement from imperial Chinese values through foreign occupation and domestic civil wars to communism and then capitalism would turn the heads of most. Without a central governing control, a defense against practical, theoretical and ideological change, any nation would have been split apart.

The central control is necessarily strong and often defends itself by copying the West. The democratically elected Senator McCarthy in the USA was allowed an autocratic pursuit of anyone with apparent communist connections, and hurt many in his zeal. Turn that practice on its head, and China's pursuit of those who apparently threaten government control, such as the Falun Gong, is understandable. What appears right at a certain time may be proved wrong later, but China is still testing the waters. In the modern United Kingdom (UK), the British police are using anti-terrorist legislation to extend powers into autocratic surveillance and the arrest of non-terrorists. Even Icelandic bank assets were seized in the UK during the credit crunch, using anti-terror laws. China happily copies such totalitarian examples of democratic penal law.

Within the legal framework of the European Union (EU), Chinese fleeing from the government are able to gain UK residency very simply. First, by any means (for example, with a visitor visa), get into the UK and go to Northern Ireland. Have a baby and apply for its citizenship under Republic of Ireland regulations (UK refuses citizenship in such visitor cases). An Irish passport, however, will be issued. Under EU regulations, the carer can apply for UK residency to look after an EU child, as any EU child may reside anywhere in the EU. China watches this in wonder and thinks to itself – no way would we let that happen, these legal human rights issues are absurdities.

The Chinese opinion of the West is therefore mixed. It sees certain democratic actions as being useful in its desire to improve itself and maintain its control over a growing and more demanding population. It also sees legislative attempts, designed to ensure that Western political desires are met, as creating unforeseen loopholes actually detrimental to those desires. The Chinese answer is to maintain flexibility in its penal law by ensuring that edicts are vague. Fit the law to the context and decide which Kafkaesque penalty to apply and when. Ignorance of the law is not a defence, but avoidance of the law, through *guanxi* connections, is quite acceptable.

The perceived authority of the West is now insufficient to command anything beyond that demanded by manners, mutual respect and reciprocity of action. China views the legislative demands of the West by, first, viewing them all with suspicion, and second, choosing only those that suit the general aims of the ruling Communist Party. Even as a signatory to the Universal Declaration of Human Rights, there is a 'pick-n-mix' attitude to its Articles. In Iraq and Guantanamo Bay, the USA seems to ignore Article 5 on torture. In China, most of Article 19 on freedom of information is subject to scrutiny. There is a 'get out' for China as a developing country – the Declaration allows for progress towards these rights. For the USA and other Western countries, the war on terror appears a regress rather than a progress.

It is poor Western behavior that quickly transforms the relationship between developed and developing nations into mutual distrust and subsequent retaliatory action. This is exemplified in the failures of Kyoto and Copenhagen to control global warming. The developed nations protected their own desires, not to control warming, but rather to retain democratic power. To place a burden on voters, such as limiting fossil fuel usage, is seen as political suicide. Just tax voters claim it is a green tax but do not otherwise limit their freedom to spend. Democracy could save the planet, but elected politicians would rather have power and taxation revenue in their pockets.

The Chinese therefore generally have a very skeptical opinion about the West and its 'holier than thou' attitude to global interaction. Now that China is a major creditor nation, it has a much stronger power base to challenge the West. It can take up opportunities to improve the lot of its people by expanding domestically, through the present recession, and can ignore demands for international change, claiming that internal affairs are its own business. Fossil fuel – coal – will continue to be a major source of its energy needs. External resource requirements will be protected by military strength and further expansion of its naval power will protect its seaboard and shipping routes. Finally, advances in its science and technology will ensure a lessening demand for US and EU assistance in health, infrastructure and computing.

Forecasting a global future

In the first decade of the twenty-first century, it is clear that the global rules have changed. The past acceleration of Chinese overseas investment is noted by the United Nations as being dominant in two areas, Africa and the Asia-Pacific region. In Africa, the advances and resource acquisition by the Chinese place China second only to South Africa; in the Asia-Pacific region, it is second only to the USA. This diversification can be looked at strategically – resource control in Africa and border control in Asia-Pacific. In other words, China is taking the opportunity to increase its overseas influence and to extend options in both areas.

It is doubtful if Chinese influences will have an adverse effect on Africa. There has been general acceptance by Africans that Chinese loans and infrastructure development are beneficial in that they are unconditional, not tied down by demands for repayment or the imposition of cultural changes. This does not mean that there is no reciprocity; quite the opposite, in fact. There is an obligation from Africa, a debt due to China. The problem for Africa is that the Chinese obligation never goes away. It remains unspecified in terms of size and timing. The future behavior of Africa will be closely monitored in Beijing. If we were to give Africa any advice it would be to repay that obligation as fast as possible. China is tying in Africa and it is cheaper to cut those ties sooner rather than later. If done quickly it would even be possible to change their nature; after all, when unspecified, an obligation is not necessarily in kind.

For the USA, however, we fear the worst. China is intent on binding relations with the richest resource hubs on the planet: close to home is Siberia, with its largely untapped treasure trove of oil and minerals; Mongolia, still a vassal state rich in copper and coal, straddles the borderlands; and somewhat further afield is the

'Irabian' Gulf with its abundant oil stream. To the south, Australia and Indonesia are key sources of minerals and liquid natural gas. Hydroelectric stations (fed by Himalayan glaciers) and coal (from dangerous pits) will provide the bulk of home-grown power generation into the 2030s. But China's greatest resource by far remains its vast population – with its energy and industry – in the realization of its global security.

The US people may be revitalized for a time by the arrival of President Barack Obama, but the factional infighting before and after the election is likely to weaken them. The fighting in Iraq and Afghanistan – the foreign wars that the US traditionally tried to avoid – have become a political means to an end. The UK's former prime minister Tony Blair may have entered Iraq hoping that Mrs Thatcher's pedestal from the Falklands would soon be under his feet – but his efforts failed. In the USA, George Bush may have entered Iraq to show that the attack on the Twin Towers of 9/11 would be avenged – but he failed. President Obama may leave Iraq claiming that Afghanistan is the final frontier – and he too will fail. Europe, of course, will argue internally and, unless it can make common cause, will also fail.

To put it bluntly, China is afraid of the democratic process, and the resulting attitude to foreign wars and domestic protection. To use domestic voters' emotions as a democratic tool to generate further domestic political power is not unusual. To use external strife to generate political power is not unusual. To create external strife to regenerate voters' emotions merely to stay in power is unforgivable. But it is not unusual.

The fear for China is that the creation of hostility against it, a simple political ruse and matched by emotional outbursts, is a clear and present possible future. The recession is the key. The emotions of the German people following the hyperinflation of the 1920s, which killed any savings, and the recession, which killed their livelihoods, were real and were manifested through the democratic process in the election of Adolf Hitler. The rest is history – but that dreadful history resulted in the invention of the nuclear bomb and its terrible use against humanity. The next war, when it comes, is already preceded by the invention and use of the bomb but also, regrettably, by its forgotten effects.

Is the future that bleak? Do we forecast China versus the USA in a nuclear shootout? 'Yes' to the first question and 'No' to the second. The future is bleak because the West has let the market run ahead of its social needs. Look again at the Declaration of Human Rights. It does not focus on preserving market economies, it concentrates on preserving society and the peoples of the world. The Declaration followed a major world war, and the war's consequences were the driving force behind it. The Declaration has now had sixty years of deadly skirmishes, with failures in Burma and Zimbabwe, in North Korea and Sudan, in North and South America, in Europe and Asia. The democratic market took over, bubbles were blown – and burst.

The global recession, however, can be a force for good by turning people away from market consumerism. And here, China should be invited to advise rather than follow – but too late. Governments in the USA and Europe have decided to encourage more spending rather than less. Market forces will fail, just as they fail regularly; capitalism is essentially destructive. These failures will force the West into a debtor position under China's sovereignty. And that will spark the China versus USA standoff already prefigured by Premier Wen.

China will certainly suffer from the recession but not, for example, as badly as Japan did in the 1990s. One market defence, and a benefit, is the *lack* of democracy in China – buying votes through over-stimulation of the economy is unnecessary. Another defence is the strong family value system in China, so that mere obedience to the government or its institutions is unlikely. Domestic and regional expansion will ease the recessionary chill – warmed by a military overcoat. The recession may be a problem for some but it is the solution that will be a problem for many. Will the world move to protect society, or will politicians move to protect their power?

Politics, opportunism, environment, might, society

> 'Tis impossible for us to carry on our inferences *in infini-tum*; and the only thing, that can stop them, is an impression of the memory or senses, beyond which there is no room for doubt or inquiry.
>
> (David Hume, *A Treatise of Human Nature*, Book I, Sect. IV)

Introduction

China is a poor country yet, paradoxically, awash with funds from every side. This accumulation of capital is unprecedented in the history of any national economy. However, Chinese banks are also valued far too high compared to their stricken Western brothers. From being public service institutions as lenders to state-owned enterprises, the banks have become conduits for the delivery of commercial lending and risk management, ostensibly to acceptable accounting and reporting standards. The greatest concern is for the quality of the assets on their balance sheets, over-inflated by cross-holdings invested in other listed Chinese companies. On the liabilities side, the true extent of bad or unrecoverable loans is masked or baldly understated.

Politically, therefore, the Chinese – like the West – will concentrate on tidying up their financial sector. But not by stimulating consumer demand – China is run by technocrats, and infrastructure development is seen as key to present employment needs and the future success of the nation. A slowdown in external demand

11

for manufactured goods is exposing Chinese overcapacity and its reliance on cheap labor (with Vietnam, Laos and Cambodia competing on low-value products). The wall of money from maternal mattresses altered the structure of the Chinese market: there are no market fundamentals by Western standards. The belief in Chinese society that the market is underwritten by the Party is persuasive and puts the Party under constant pressure from its people.

Chinese governmental strategy depends upon balancing the tension between domestic societal needs with the market stimulus needed to preserve that society. The balance is a cleft stick with two messages: social stability versus economic uncertainty. In some respects, China has recognized what the West has lost: the need for some type of equilibrium between society and market. How does China, firmly entrenched in the communal family adapt to a capitalist market? Simply, by trial and error but governed by an overwhelming sense that failure could lead to chaos.

China, it must be remembered, leapfrogs over problems into the future – knocking down mistakes and setting up the next. The West consolidates as it goes, creating cracks but papering them over to hide the disasters. The primary difference between these two practices will result, structurally, in China being stronger and the West weaker. China also manages the gymnastic feat of going forward while looking back (remember the futuristic Olympic opening ceremony with its Confucian, not communist, overtones) and is counting down to its imperial past at the centre of the world.

China's most recent past has been incredibly unstable but still defines its present, and from the present is where its future must start. In some respects, China's desire to avoid further instability can make its actions appear overly totalitarian inside China and yet unnecessarily 'standoffish' when external problems, such as those emanating from North Korea, Burma (Myanmar) and Darfur, demand intervention. Part I, therefore, sets the scene for an understanding of China's external positioning, its internal protection, and its border policing.

Executive summary

This first part contends that the West and China have opposing value and belief systems. Much of Part I is a summary and update of our previous book, *China Calling*. The world has changed dramatically since its publication in 2008, but its foundations, its historical behavioral patterns, have not. How we react to new problems is shaped by our experience of past ones. Economic believers in J. M. Keynes will stimulate to succeed but quantitative easing is not the Chinese way. Infrastructure development can now be brought forward and lead to a modern China while the West eases into any economic recovery by increasing taxes and fighting inflation. There is a major difference in the politics, opportunistic behavior, environment, might and its uses and societal templates that guide the two factions of the globe. Understanding that difference should help to ease the present mutual mistrust and lessen global tension. The following sections in Part I are aimed at explaining the difference:

1. *Politics* explains China's progress towards the internal integration of its people's mandate for stability and security. The changing attitude of the ruling Communist Party to external adaptation is profiled.

2. *Opportunism* is a common practice for China's expansion into the world order, and is illustrated as a balanced desire for market forces and resources to accept the societal needs of a growing and more demanding population.

3. *Environment* is an encompassing term for the holistic approach that China takes to problems requiring solutions to economic growth, but without the destruction of people's health and welfare.

4. *Might* and its uses are Party solutions to resolve China's demand for internal pacification and external border control, and for security of transport and communication channels.

5. *Society* is all-important in China's internal Party struggles. The nature of Chinese history is revolutionary rather than democratic. Imperial rules dictated a strong but civil Civil Service: a service to and for the people by the emperor, and a mandate

from Heaven that must be beneficial, not brutal. The Party is the new lieutenant of the imperial command and is continuing in its change from policing the people to leading the nation. Its mandate, however, needs continuing massage, and we discuss whether an increasing number of foreign and internal crises are prompting more rebels in Chinese society to take action.

Part I therefore brings the reader up to date with China as it stands in 2009.

CHAPTER 1

Politics

This realm, half-shadowed, China's empery.
(Camoens, *The Luciad X.181*)

Introduction

In March, 2009, the Chinese Communist Party (the Party) decided on its political position for the next set of budgets, and the next set of strategies for retaining power. The crises of 2007 and 2008 have been much worse in their global repercussions than the failure of a few Western banks could have foretold: Chinese factories closed rapidly and a return to the fields and to family elders by migrant workers is commonplace. Particularly hard hit is southern China, with factory redundancies in their thousands. Closed factories have reversed the past rapid growth in Hong Kong's exports and booming container trades. Ships that carried those cargoes are now anchored around the islands that dot the Pearl River delta – awaiting orders.

But orders are few and far between. Contracts are being rewritten. Relationships are fraying. A lack of positive growth makes democracy, as the West understands it, difficult to introduce. The Party is becoming protectionist and well-known figures are keeping their peace. This makes any form of electoral reform difficult. The Chinese work with those they know. If you do not know a candidate for power, why vote for him or her? Even worse, having previously protected themselves from imperial control, why throw that protection away with an electoral registration? And actually voting where the ballot is traceable (as in the UK) to the individual voter on the electoral list, is surely impossible in a low-trust country? Democracy depends on trust and that is an elusive, often frail, construct in modern global politics. In China, trust in someone you have not met is almost non-existent.

With the collapse of the commune system and the closing of most of the state-owned enterprises, peasant farmers and farmhands are thrown back on their own resources and have to fend for themselves. This is clearly difficult with little or no recourse to other sources of income. They can just about scratch a living from the land they inhabit, but without another activity – sale of handicrafts, local crops and fruit – life is extremely hard, often quite desperate. As a result, farm workers all over China can often only meet land taxes by further reducing their ancestral holdings. The damage caused to the politically disenfranchised masses, by turning farmland into factories, is now coming back to haunt the Party. Social stability is seen as being linked to, but more important than, economic growth. Even village voting for better representation is constrained by intimidatory advice on the consequences of marking any but the official candidate's box. Fear is overcoming traditional *guanxi* protection. Not a good democratic omen.

The West, however, has traditionally trusted its legal and regulatory systems, but even they are now under considerable scrutiny. Their past failures are well publicized. Protection from the chill winds of recession rests, for all, with the family. The Chinese have always relied on their relationships for help and assistance and, as global complexity increases, these relationships remain effective but are undergoing stress tests. Past Western demands for strong legal systems are not being ignored, but are being postponed. The Chinese are not copying all Western institutional controls; they are deliberately avoiding the difficult ones. Their basic strategy, their solution to future uncertainty, is a 'pick-n-mix' strategy. Just as the West might feel it can ignore UN resolutions if it feels like having a foreign war, so the Chinese will also turn their blind eye to legal precedents. Rules are chosen as and when they are needed.

The problem

This change in Chinese political characteristics has not received the studied Western attention it merits. Chinese strategies, for example, allow remnants of communist planning to survive, and recent experience indicates that there has been much trial and error reform. Legal systems change slowly, and arbitration provides a handy midway point for the Chinese. Why should the world go West when, as George Orwell pointed out, 'it's an eccentricity to be white'? That eccentricity is now well established as a failure in world governance. The West must now recognize itself as an equal player in the global game.

The West points to disruptions in geographic and cultural clashes within China, but does not recognize them simply as divergences between tribes. Chinese farmers know their local land ownership, and the building developers know local political power. It is the clash of tribal networks, not of civilizations, that defines friction in China. The disturbances in Tibet certainly foment fear and anger – on both sides. In mid-March 2008, the foreign news services, such as the BBC and CNN, were jammed by the Chinese authorities, and pictures of suppression were prevented from reaching residents in China.

Paradoxically, in preventing insurrection against the state, China is following international precedents and international law. Tibet is logically accepted as being internal to China (as is Taiwan since the USA finally acknowledged Beijing in 1978) and it is how, not why, the disturbances are quelled that is the issue. Yet Tibetan supporters, in disturbing the Greek Olympic representative, Mynos Kyriakou, at the Athens Olympic flame ceremony, did themselves no favours – they allow China to show why Tibet needs controlling.

It is the external drip into China that fires the Chinese mind, the 'do not meddle in my affairs' attitude. We did not interfere in Northern Ireland, nor in Iraq, nor in Grenada, nor in other parts of the world that are not our internal concern, the Chinese cry. Where we trade is another matter from where we politicize. The Dalai Lama recognizes this and exhorts the world to engage with China to stop the Han Chinese control in Tibet. It is the fear of China on the tribal doorstep that fires extremism.

That fear, though, has now spread to the USA. Fears that China will control American debt continue to grow unabated. US debt, from an American perspective, has raced past the Chinese to become a global issue. There is an unstable equilibrium in the global economy – a shift to the East. And with fear comes emotional decision-making. Protectionism in the West is denied but is in hand. Market forces, the West cries, were fine but only when it suited us. Uncontrolled open markets have damaged the West, so Western central banks control their own free capitalist banks – just like China controls its free state-owned enterprises, especially its banks.

Political management is advancing rapidly in a region that is still shaking off past colonial shackles and post-war communist ideals, a region that is undergoing shocks to its domestic systems as it adjusts to global ways of doing things. The major regional force to be reckoned with is that of China and Chinese values. That force can be channeled, with the West providing help rather than hindrance. Hindrance is interference in their 'internal affairs'.

Internal affairs

In the lead up to the return of Hong Kong to China in 1997, negotiations were often frayed, with attempts at democracy in Hong Kong being treated by China as insulting. Open democratic freedoms had not been extended under British rule but there was a mad rush to put them in place before the handover. The negotiations were terse but always ended with the diplomatic phrase 'useful and constructive'. Strangely, that is always true no matter the nature of the negotiations. It is only at the end of the negotiations when the deal is done that the statement can be seen to be true or false, constructive or destructive. But negotiations are always useful. China, however, draws a line between internal and external negotiations. Internal negotiations are not to be interfered with nor pressured by external political statements.

The Chinese National Congress emphasizes harmony as a communist ideal and a necessary societal influence – somewhat stronger than that brought to bear by Capitol Hill's lobbyists, or bureaucrats in Brussels. It is the pandering to Western voters by the political parties of the West, the grandstanding to the public, the search for power through the ballot box that China finds reprehensible and hypocritical.

Is democracy just possibly a mental space, inhabited partly by those who see it as a *realpolitik* distraction to keep dissidents preoccupied, and partly by those who see it as a Western failure in governance? The answer – in a very guarded and qualified way from official Chinese sources off the record – is an unequivocal 'yes'. There are several immovable, non-negotiable issues which stand as roadblocks to more democratic freedoms. These are, in order of intractability: recognition of human rights; Taiwan; Tibet; and Xinjiang autonomy.

Taiwan and Tibet remain intractable borders of control for China. Potential conflict with Taiwan is now averted by the Kuomintang's (KMT's) victory in the March 2008 election. KMT policy is to establish direct links with the mainland, building closer relations and a 'common market' to help revive Taiwan's faltering economy. It also seeks a formal peace treaty, paving the way for Taiwan's accommodation as a quite different special administrative region. The USA sees Tibet as a chance to attack China, while China points out US hypocrisy on torture and human rights, especially at Guantanamo Bay. A future stand-off between the two great nations is likely. China will only talk to those who recognize its borders and territories as integral parts of the country. But Xinjiang is the last stop before the Muslim steppes – a border between Han and Islam, clearly demarcated in the riots of 2009.

Both Taiwan and China recognize, at the internal political level, that there is only one China, but that its nature is dual. There will be some types of alliance, already working economically, which should allow an accommodation at the diplomatic and ultimately at the political level. Not so for Tibet. There is, in Chinese eyes, a clear support for secession by Western countries, with France and Germany most recently bearing the brunt of Chinese anger at their welcoming of the Dalai Lama. Tibet is, however essential to China's energy plans – a source of both water and wind power – and will suffer increased oppression if it looks likely that trouble is increasing. An understanding of Chinese border control and an engagement with China is more likely to help Tibetans rather than any inflammatory actions overseas.

Fearing trouble in Tibet during the fiftieth anniversary of the take-over by China – the oxymoronic 'democratic reform' anniversary – the Chinese ensured an armed police crackdown in early 2009. There is a continuing fear of a lack of stability spilling over into neighboring regions. Xinjiang, for example, had a mix of religions before becoming mainly Muslim; there were Persian influences such as Zoroastrianism, and Buddhism was the major religion 2,000 years ago. In some respects, the growth of Islam was tempered by Tibetan Buddhist influences linking Xinjiang to Tibet. Xinjiang remains a religious thorn in the Western flank of China.

The Party will therefore maintain its strict border controls and policing of practices and religions that might threaten their control over China's development. At present it is very difficult to foresee any serious political systemic change in China's internal affairs for ten to twenty years, almost a generation. The management of this change is based on a fairly straightforward social pact between Party and citizen: if you don't support the Party, you can say goodbye to economic prosperity. Both the Party and the people are scared of a *da luan*, a great chaos that could result from economic and territorial collapse and the subsequent revolt and vengeance of the masses.

China sees a similar problem for chaos in the West, but from the vengeance of the new middle classes rather than from the old poor. Those who saved and are now in poverty, those who went for the American dream and are now in poverty, those who see Wall Street as protected but Main Street as open to the desert winds, are all suffering. Is democratic choice sufficiently robust to handle depression? The Chinese doubt it.

The world is too unstable to allow democracy a free rein. Total control, preferably centralized, is needed. The IMF, the World Bank, the UN and the WTO are all globally strong institutions but are not sufficiently powerful to ensure that credit markets are maintained in an open and transparent way for developing countries. Cash is going into the capitalist banking systems. China could, almost single-handed, assist the developing world – but at the cost of and loss to the West. Fortunately for the West, but unfortunately for the developing world, China will never actively seek involvement in the 'internal affairs' of others because, as explained earlier, China does not want any interference within its own borders.

Traditional values – honoring of ancestors and striving through education to advance the family's standing – are embedded in a tribal and clan way of life. They have re-emerged vigorously after many decades of suppression. Mao outlawed Confucianism as being feudal, and the Party line is still that all religion is superstition.

There have been cases, for example, of US messianic zeal easily converting overseas Chinese on educational programs in the USA to Christianity. Beijing then quickly switched government training courses to the less evangelical UK. State atheism is used much as the Nazis used it in Germany, to create an ideology of invincibility in war, or by the French revolutionaries to overthrow their monarchy and establish an entirely new order of absolute equality and justice before the law of mankind.

State atheism is based on the fear that religion (particularly foreign, imported religion) will weaken and dissipate the Party's authority. The reality is that the theories of Party dogma have become quite detached from the ancient practices of the people. What this means is that the real power to move people to action and to order the outcome of events is reverting to the village headmen and clan leaders. These are the officials who will settle local disputes through the authority vested in them from control of ancestral temples and shrines. The Party has progressively cut back taxes as a gesture of appeasement to the people. Thrown back on their own resources, local authorities are developing a spirit of entrepreneurialism to help them replace these revenues. Local temple authorities and clan associations are the first lines of recourse for this reformation.

This is an era of integrated but controlled religion, which the Party now finds convenient not to discourage. The Falun Gong movement and the Christian Church are still held in great suspicion and closely monitored. The numbers of their followers are rising and producing precious mental oxygen in a country where people are accustomed not to breathe too deeply for fear of inhaling either toxins or persecution. The fresh air and space created by these forced measures of personal autonomy are restoring to the Chinese people their natural stoicism and initiative. Such internal change is happening, but in a systemic fashion – through trial and error and without external interference.

The solution lies overseas

The new generation of Chinese leaders are those who went overseas in the first period of reform from 1978, mainly as students and visiting scholars to Europe and the USA, but retaining strong basic human values. There is some similarity between Christian ethics and Confucian moral guidance. The difference between the moral value systems – and it is a big difference – is that Western ethics are based on the individual doing what their personal conscience believes is right, while Confucian morality depends on the individual doing what the group believes is harmonious. Western values are shaped largely by a sense of individual guilt; while Chinese values are driven largely by an anxiety to avoid group shame.

Chinese leaders understand this, but the West tends to ignore it. Individual rights are not the same as group rights. They intersect, of course, as rather different notions of honor and integrity. Harmony within a community is important. The Chinese do not enshrine any form of human rights legislation. How can it be enforced? Group behavior is self-correcting and so is group economic behavior – unless the groups are of opposing nations. Chinese controls govern Chinese group behavior.

It is the group versus the individual that sets the differences between East and West. The economics of the West are based on rational beings, the individual acting in his or her own self-interest (so well argued by the Scottish free trader, Adam Smith), creating the communal 'invisible hand' of the market. Unfortunately, Smith also pointed out that the invisible hand is often challenged by the individual seeking to better the market. That is why Western individualistic rational man failed in Japan. He will also fail in China. Chinese economic strategies are very long-term. The Chinese leadership is turning its trading and manufacturing expertise into a market economy, but this economy is based on collectivist, not communist (or capitalist) ideals. Chinese economic management must eventually clash with the West's. Chinese economic behavior has not changed under different governmental structures and, as Francis Fukuyama points out, is 'in some sense a natural outgrowth of Sinitic culture'.

The Chinese surplus has outgrown its own borders and has moved overseas. Partial offsets of this surplus are the purchase of US Treasury Bonds (nearly US$1 trillion held in 2009, with the Japanese holding a little under US$700 billion) and further diversification of its foreign exchange reserves into currencies other than the US dollar, such as sterling and the euro. China also moved overseas into a 'sovereign fund' of state investment shareholdings and forays into private equity via investment firms – a disastrous series of investments given the poor governance of the Western banking system. However, these are at present small adjustments compared with the real investment lines being laid down in Africa, the Middle East and Latin America.

In Africa, China established special economic zones in Nigeria, Tanzania, Zambia and Mauritius, clusters for Chinese companies, with import duties and tax incentives designed to induce these companies to set up permanent bases on the continent. Large amounts are also being poured into infrastructure. At a conference in 2008 with African leaders in Beijing, one African beneficiary claimed that the money came with no strings attached – 'If there are, I can't see them, maybe they're made of nylon.' In Latin America, Chinese direct investment accounts for over one-third of its overall direct investment worldwide – chiefly in Brazil (railways, low-cost housing, communications and satellites), Venezuela (oil production) and Argentina (infrastructure). And the investments are, of course, politically directed. Political direction is also provided in the trading of currencies, as the Chinese fear of the US dollar weakening is driving bilateral exchange. The Brazilian real is being traded for the Chinese renminbi, bypassing the US dollar as an intermediate trade, strengthening the Brazil/China relationship and weakening Western influence in Latin America.

Contagion at the border

When Shanghai sneezed in the spring of 2007, the instability in Western financial markets revealed a poor immune system. A minor market, ramped and rampant, causing global fright? Could the sophistication of Western hedging systems, of computerized arbitrage, of incredibly expensive fund managers, count for so little? Can the West be that vulnerable, dependent on Chinese fiscal decision-making and taxi-driver punts for market direction? Is genius in short financial supply or is it measured erroneously by Wall Street bankers' bonuses? Apparently, genius was never there in the first place, just the bonuses.

When the US subprime market caused the Western capitalist rules to fail, then Western central banks stepped in. Capitalism's open markets and loosely regulated activities are examples of Western ways that are not applicable to the opportunistic and secretive Chinese. Can China not remain a global workhouse keeping Western electorates with low attention spans sweet with cheap consumables? The Chinese dream is diverse but it does not include foreigners, their chaotic markets and *post hoc* regulatory controls. Control of China, by China, and for China, is a central policy of Beijing.

Of course, Asia does have its foreigners; its own diversity. There is considerable variety in the characteristics and habits of mind of the East Asian peoples. In Europe also, considerable variety exists across borders – the Germans, Italians and Finns, for example, have very different languages and cultural identities. However, the strong thread that binds the political and trading tapestries in East Asia is identifiably Chinese. Local Asian governments know this but may not admit it. Their problems are primarily those of cohesion – keeping the indigenous population under control – and their problems increase in inverse ratio to stock market valuations. Race riots are not the sole preserve of Los Angeles.

As both Western and Asian protectionism increases, we believe that China will become embroiled in anti-Chinese sentiment in Asia. The sparks will be North Korea and the Bahasa speakers of Muslim Malaysia/Indonesia. Both feel threatened by Chinese influence. Malaysian democratic elections in 2008 continue to cause concern to the ruling Bumiputra, who see local ethnic Chinese (and Indian) votes as challenging. The Japanese may continue to suffer from historical mistrust but they do not make up an important component of overseas populations (except perhaps in Hawaii and Peru). Jealousy of Chinese trading abilities elsewhere in Asia (and Wall Street) will increase with political support for regional expansion, backed by at least the threat of military pressure, emanating from Beijing. Taiwan cross-strait recognition is another major step on the road to consolidating Chinese power.

Therefore, regionalization, not globalization, is the prime political challenge for the Party. We must remember that the Chinese government and state-owned enterprises are run, in the main, by engineering graduates. The political approach is very mechanistic and often keeps the old engineers' trick of at least a 10 per cent safety margin in any design, appointing sociologists, lawyers and economists where the machinery of government needs strengthening. In other words, Chinese diplomacy is not one of smooth words and soft actions. It is often calculated with slide rule precision and if it means brinkmanship then it will be brinkmanship with something up the sleeve. Gnawing slowly away at the problem will ultimately bring the solution. But it will be a solution based on equilibrium. Do not tell the Chinese to do something that you would not do yourself (a Confucian refrain). So do not invade Iraq and tell China to leave Tibet. Chinese policy is practical and primarily regional.

It is here that the West is worried. The large state-owned investment entities have been accepted as wise investors – Kuwaitis, Norwegians and others have used sovereign wealth funds to recycle petrodollars. But China, through the China Investment Corporation, plays by different rules. It is recycling imported dollars in a non-transparent way and possibly in a speculative manner. Again, Western hypocrisy comes to the fore. Opaque hedge funds are acceptable, whereas opaque Chinese sovereign funds are not. Despite assurances from the Chinese prime minister that any investment into global companies from China's sovereign wealth fund would meet transparency and corporate governance requirements, uneasiness remains about the potential extent of such incursions. In fact, the sum available for such investment is not nearly as great as it first appears, since much of the fund (more than one third) is likely to be spent in China itself on the very necessary and urgent reform of China's commercial banking system.

Two points of principle must be made to explain the concerns. First, the retention of relational controls in a Chinese organization with a hierarchical reporting and response structure does not comply with Western legal governance for corporate responsibility. Second, market reliance on shareholding as a financial investment (buy low and sell high) does not create true stakeholders. In large Chinese listed companies, the state is the only controlling stakeholder (think Bank of China and its tax rebates, and its waivers on bad loan provisions). In any entrepreneurial publicly listed companies, the controlling family is the stakeholder (think Li Ka-Shing, or the Australian–American–Asian Rupert Murdoch).

Western constitutions and legal systems enshrine and safeguard the rights of the individual. The key provisions made have evolved from the principles of morality, justice, equity (or fairness) and pluralism, which form the basis of the common law. Notions such as equality before the law and *habeas corpus* – which requires anyone detained or arrested to have a legal hearing before further detention or imprisonment – have their British roots in the Magna Carta of 1215 and are the bedrock of values, legal precedent and case law governing the behavior of individuals in society.

Although democracy is based on the rule of law and allows a government to govern only with the consent of the people, abuses of power are quite common, precisely because the existence of power is a matter of law, not of fact. Thus, the corruption of friendship may subvert the system, since public office-holders have natural emotional controls as well as social legal personalities. Individuals need recourse not just to legal redress – which may take some time and be expensive – but, more urgently and more importantly, to a very present help in times of trouble, which the Chinese culture provides.

The best example of this dilemma with Western legal process is probably the Madoff case in the USA. Rich individuals were apparently duped through qualitative assurances (very Chinese) at social and sporting clubs into believing that the investment fund manager Bernard Madoff could make you a solid return no matter the state of the market. Smell a rat? The statement attributed to Abraham Lincoln that 'You can fool some of the people all of the time, and all of the people some of the time, but you cannot fool all of the people all of the time' seems to have caught up with Madoff. The rich, famous and wealthy (including fund managers who played with the money of the not-so-rich) did not act with due diligence. They became some of the people all of the time. But did the regulatory and legal system of the West protect them from their foolhardiness? Of course not! The West is just as penal as the Chinese legal system except that Madoff gets life behind bars and Chinese crooks get eternal life below ground.

In China there exists a protective system of networks where one does not deal with anyone who is not deemed trustworthy. The network system of *guanxi* means, effectively, practical recourse through particular people to a possible solution to a problem – in the English sense of 'using connections'. But in its binding power of obligation, it has the socially institutional force of law. Its use is never based simply on an altruistic granting or exchange of favours. It is always based on anticipated reciprocation in roughly equal measure or value (with interest) on some unspecified future occasion. It is the essence of Chinese political negotiation, it is *renqing*, the human obligation, that governs the deal making.

The action and spirit of these networks are well encapsulated in China's perception of its own soft power in the world. The country sees the main concern in international relations shifting to and from military and territorial issues, and between economic and trading issues. It recognizes that the rate and impact of interdependence in the international networked economy is increasing. It firmly believes that in making strategic moves it will be part of a framework discussed in a reciprocal fashion with its global partners. It is for the West to recognize that China relies on networked reciprocity if China is needed to reduce instability in the world.

About face?

In the aftermath of the 2008 Olympics in Beijing and the run-up to the Expo in Shanghai in 2010, China presents a smiling, accommodating face. It will now begin to assert itself forcefully through its relational power, with a hardening of its negotiating stance on trade and human rights issues. Fewer concessions can be expected by the USA and the EU in any extensive revaluation of the renminbi (at least once the Chinese currency absorbs the Hong Kong dollar, fixed by the British in the 1980s at 7.8 HK dollars to the US dollar), liberalization of financial markets, trade quotas and market access and entry by foreign firms. Protectionism in the West reinforces China's global stand: protectionist rules are equitable to all! It may simply be a question of who blinks first.

But China will still have a point. The Triennial Central Bank Survey for 2007 indicates that the daily turnover in global foreign exchange markets was in excess of US$3 trillion. There is no way that such daily turnover was related to trade in anything beyond currencies themselves. Indeed, the Central Bank figures show that spot trades are much less than forward swaps and derivatives, with the latter making up more than half of the daily turnover. How easily will China give up its currency to hedge funds' forward positions? The Asian currency crisis of 1997 was not so long ago, it still rankles, and suspicion is reinforced by the 2008 Wall Street debacle. The Chinese currency will not strengthen under speculative forces but the Chinese government will gradually engineer a continuing but slow increase in the renminbi versus the US dollar.

China had a bad experience of the West in the nineteenth and twentieth centuries, and there remains a deep-seated feeling that reparations are in order to redress the damage done. Public opinion in the country will remain squarely behind the government's efforts to defend national interests and uphold national pride at any price. The country is now unashamedly mercantilist in its trade ambitions – and this political strategy is designed to benefit itself, not its trading partners. Its currency exchange rate gives it a massive advantage, underpinning production, exports and jobs. It is looking to engage mainly with foreign companies that will bring it innovative processes to advance its technology swiftly, enhance its export-driven industries, and provide jobs, particularly in rural and inland areas. If the foreign companies do not buy into China, then China will buy into them.

But it depends how you buy into China. Buying a famous brand – such as the attempt by Coca-Cola to buy Huiyuan fruit juice drinks company in 2009 – is not the same as righting the failures of a smaller enterprise or expanding a small to medium enterprise (SME) into a multinational enterprise (MNE). The US press complains that disallowing large purchases is detrimental to China's growth. US allegations of Chinese brand protection arise whilst some argue that it is tit-for-tat because of the past US denial of the oil company Unocal to China. We disagree. This is China saying that it does not need buyouts of successful brands and companies – it does not need cash. China needs growth investment and seed money accompanied by new technology.

Political direction

Directed protectionism always plays a part in Chinese politics. That applies also to Chinese Party cadres. *Xinhua* news agency reported, in early 2009 from Beijing, that Wu Bangguo, chairman of the Standing Committee of the People's National Congress, confirmed that China will 'never simply copy the Western model'. The phrasing is important. It reinforces the Chinese stance that a pragmatic, protective, pick-n-mix strategy is their way forward. If it works, we'll use it, they say, but for the moment, as the Western model does not seem to be working very well, there is no hurry to adopt it.

There is scant likelihood that China will move in the direction of Korean- or Taiwan-style democratization in the short-to-medium term. Because of tough thought-control in the media and with continuing restricted internet access, the vast majority of Chinese are quite ill-informed about the true nature and state of affairs outside China. Thus they lack a sufficient basis of comparison to determine the merits and advantages of any alternative form of government. Even with free choice, who can defend the prostitution of Western political parties to big business, to spin and vote-buying, to lobby groups? Trading votes for money is illegal, but buying political clout is only a matter of interpretation. Perhaps it is Western-style democracy, not Chinese-style communism that is the true illusion.

A snapshot of the country towards the end of the first decade of the twenty-first century looks something like this: the centre ground is held by the president in his charmed circle of nominal power, within which he is expected to orchestrate the direction of the economy. In fact, he has extremely limited room for maneuver within this designated space without in some way widening the scope of his mandate to draw to himself from civil society some real power and authority to act. Against him is ranged the army like a huge potential landslip. They rely on his patronage, as do Party cadres, to maintain their wealth, property and business activities.

This bizarre balance of totalitarian socialism with laissez-faire capitalism is highly precarious and the major cause of chronic tension and uncertainty within the current regime. The Old Guard of retired generals and Party members, as well as the young princelings, the rising heirs of Party cadres and thus of natural privilege, are mired in the machinations and plottings of an almost medieval statecraft. The old leaders' genes live on with descendants of Mao Zedong, Zhou Enlai and Deng Xiaoping represented at the 2009 National People's Congress. The Party is aiming at internal future stability through the formation of communist dynasties!

The real Grand Question that is now posed is this: how on earth is this dynastic tension and uncertainty to be eased without some gradual systemic shift towards legitimizing the dissent and opposition of the dispossessed and disenfranchised in China – which will otherwise fester and ferment into even more uncontainable revolt and further rebellion? The answer, of course, lies in the area of greatest paradox: how to reconcile the burning patriotism every Chinese person feels with the feelings of hatred provoked by the impasse of fear, a fear of losing control over personal destiny. In short, how can China create and enfranchise a loyal opposition and stop treating dissenters as enemies of the state?

This will require the most extraordinary moral courage from Chinese intellectuals – whose fear is still a palpable obstacle to progress in this direction. Intellectuals, from Socrates and Galileo to Luther and Solzhenitsyn, so many of them latterly supine over Katyn Wood and the Cambodian killing fields, cowed, compliant or heroic in the McCarthy and Maoist purges, have only been brave sporadically. Human nature is human nature – fear will cause the head to be withdrawn below the parapet. But it is not just the Chinese fear of systemic chaos that is so present and alarming. It is its spatial predecessor, a messing up of the old order, a *mélange* of half-baked rules and confusing time-spans that mixes old systems with new, that has already arrived.

Political tension

We argue that the hidden levers of power in China are being subjected to such unprecedented stresses and strains in recent years that traditional *guanxi* network mechanisms have warped and been forced to adapt in accommodating new pressures from below. The groundswell and sway of public opinion, the seesaw of influence, is tilting in favor of those who are being left behind – chiefly the inland rural poor whose near destitution in the wake of the great surges in coastal prosperity is already the focus of continuous, unresolved unrest. The Party is now very much alive to the gaping disparity in the distribution of new wealth and attempts to address this by infrastructure packages allocated primarily to greater access between rural and urban centers.

Party officials define their own terms of supposedly hierarchical rights and percentages of entitlement, while the rural peasantry use it to describe the bonds of extended family and ancestral land roots and usage. Whose is the more just and rightful claim? Here lies the rub, and the dilemma. The sop of partial dispensation from paying local taxes is hardly sufficient compensation for loss of ancient titles to land, when housing, transport and education costs make the unequal burden of living almost unsupportable. Once the economy is marketized, then the price of this land bubbles way beyond the meager means of landed peasants to repossess it as their own, and their sense of dispossession grows mordantly keen. The benefit of the recession is therefore the reinforcement of the links with ancestral land. As factories closed in Southern China, the migrant jobless returned to farms and fields, to raise chickens and grow rice. Lower land prices are now paying off in smallholding sustenance.

Yet when Ernst & Young, the Western accounting company, pointed out that China's massive foreign exchange reserves could be said to have been eclipsed by the total volume of its bad bank loans, amounting to roughly the same figure, the Chinese were moved beyond mere indignation into outrage by this aberrant assertion, claiming that, since cash was a circulating medium it should be channeled wherever it could best lubricate the economy. This answer seemed communist a couple of years prior to the financial crisis, but now seems eminently sensible. It is not what you measure that matters but when you measure it. This demonstrated yet again, in a peculiarly forthright way, how measure and degree are largely relative matters in China.

Chinese democracy

China's definition of democracy is this: 'The Chinese Communist party governing on behalf of the people ... while upholding and perfecting the people's democratic dictatorship'. It is, of course, a splendid piece of nonsense, an exquisite oxymoron – almost as good as 'the dictatorship of the proletariat' itself. China is shadow boxing with its demons – oxymorons creating the harmonious choice of referee. Perhaps the Chinese definition of democracy is no less valid than the English writer Alan Coren's rather more accurate and concise argument: 'Democracy consists of choosing your dictators, after they've told you what it is you want to hear.'

The notion of dictatorship being in some way perfectible is particularly aberrant, since by definition it is rule by the will of the one individual, not of the many. It is ridiculous, a travesty of the concept of concord or harmony, this imposition of a collective cast of mind on the thinking and behavior of an entire people. The supreme irony is that the Greek philosopher Plato was no champion of democracy, regarding it as corrupt and inefficient. He thought that the best government was by a philosopher king with a court of wisest advisers – roughly what the current Chinese leadership apparently aspires to.

Their problem is that, having done away with their emperor (and very nearly with Confucius as well), the Chinese leadership is made up of technocrats who are visionary on structures but somewhat short of the spirit of free enquiry and debate. This is why they fear democracy, because it could produce chaos, with people claiming that they know what is best for them and, goodness gracious, demanding autonomy, argument and choice – in other words something beyond the passing contentment brought on by shopping for consumer goods.

Certainly, the politicians boldly assert that the country would not suffer anything but a minor slowdown. In the face of a 20 per cent increase in fixed-asset investment to hasten industrialization and modernization, this would be reasonable. There is a clear desire for China to become the second-largest world economy, supplanting Japan, in the years after 2009. The Party is right in terms of basic economic definitions, but what exactly does a large economy mean? It surely means that society benefits as well as the national coffers, not just by infrastructure spending and high production levels, but by fair and equitable social values. Economists often produce arguments on what causes an economy to grow, but do not often get the moral reasons correct. Economists and politicians massage figures to avoid accusations of linking their reasoning to previous events merely because those events happened earlier. To accurately predict we need solid, robust thinking which reflects society's needs, not scholarly assumptions of theoretical market forces.

And thinking is always massaged by politicians. In his speech to the 17th Party Congress in October 2007, President Hu mentioned 'democracy' no fewer than sixty times. It has become a weasel word, a kind of decoy or shield against criticism in the tortuous process of the Party's political evolution and internal reform towards allowing a very gradual participation so far denied even to lower-ranking members, not to mention the people. As in ancient Greece, fully three-quarters (and more) of the people remain excluded from participatory government. The party elite are the only true 'citizens'; the rest of the people remain effectively, as in Athens of old, the disenfranchised 'slaves'. The country remains in an intractable bind of mutual suspicion, fear and contained anger between government and governed, not too dissimilar to Confucian times. And, dare we say it, not too distant from present Western democracies. Politically both West and East are facing similar problems.

The Party Congress therefore addressed the problems as they saw them, with *China Daily – Xinhua* commenting on Premier Wen's remarks on March 14, 2009:

- Stimulus – we have enough ammunition to increase fiscal spending, with 4 trillion renminbi (US$590 billion) allocated.

- Confidence – is more important than gold or money and the Chinese people must warm the economy with his or her warm heart (*sic*).

- Foreign exchange – a huge amount of capital is loaned to the USA and we are, to speak truthfully, a little bit worried. Others must not put pressure on our currency.

- Growth target – a target of 8 per cent is possible with effort, but no matter how much is given to the countryside it is still insufficient.

- Tibet – some Western countries exploit the Dalai Lama, and their behavior harms the feelings of the Chinese people.

- Taiwan – I would like to go to Taiwan.

- Fiscal deficit – our level of debt is in the safety zone.

- G20 meetings – China will help the least developed countries

Imagine telling a Western democracy that the economy will warm through the warm hearts of the voters! With half of its reserves in the USA, it is not surprising that China is worried, as a quick look at the US Treasury system shows (see Table I.1).

Table I.1 US Treasury securities

Major foreign holders of Treasury securities	In billions of US$ June 2009	Approx annual growth 2008–9 (%)
China	776	45
Japan	712	13
United Kingdom	214	83
Oil exporters	191	19
Caribbean banking centers	190	77
Brazil	140	−12
Russia	120	17

Source: US Dept of Treasury (www.treas.gov/tic/mfh.txt).

The USA thus has a problem not just with China. Tax havens and the Russians are now holding a fair amount of US debt. From a total US debt of US$3.4 trillion (up 30 per cent in one year) the seven holders shown in Table I.1 account for 70 per cent of the total – not a very comforting mix for the democratic USA. Yet it is a mix that shows a shaky confidence in where to put the savings of several of the world's non-democracies.

There is thus a continuing desire for confidence in the USA, demonstrated at the G20 summit in April 2009. From a political standpoint, China probably succeeded the most. It had no announced agenda but came to listen. If the West would listen to its democracies then its politicians might have a better grasp of what is required by society. However, political hypocrisy remains high.

Notwithstanding the G20 demands to close down tax havens, the US Treasury has happily issued Caribbean bankers with US$190 billion of securities (see Table I.1). The substantial rise in UK-held US Treasury securities reflects London's position as a global financial center for overseas investors, not necessarily as a haven for overseas tax avoidance. The actual UK resident-held US securities are probably about US$50 billion.

If we had to summarize the primary political differences between Western democracies and Chinese communism we would wonder why the money and effort spent on political party canvassing (look at Obama's cash requirements to win the US Democratic nomination and then the presidential election) could not be better used for the nation. Europe has its entrenched historical infighting and murky allegations – Italy has the beloved Berlusconi, France had Chirac and Germany had Kohl. The UK has sleaze. The Western democracies can be interpreted, to paraphrase President Abraham Lincoln, as *governing the people by a party for the power*. The Chinese are more pragmatic, *governing a people by the Party for a purpose*. There is a clear unification principle in China, and that principle will always be politically and militarily stronger when set against a divided, albeit democratic, West.

CHAPTER 2

Opportunism

For whether the passion of self-interest be esteemed vicious or virtuous, 'tis all a case; since itself alone restrains it.

(David Hume, *A Treatise of Human Nature*,
Book III, Sect. II)

Introduction

The 2008 credit crunch and cash write-offs had early warning signals, from the HSBC 2006 subprime problems in the USA to the Shanghai stock market drop in early 2007. Global linkages create perspectives not previously anticipated by North American and European business. The capitalist difficulties in the West allow the Chinese to nod knowingly that the 'foreign moon is not more round'. Rational thinking in the East and West is asymmetrical, yet because something is foreign we all tend to assume that it is better or worse than our homespun values. The Chinese see their values as more attuned to fluctuations in economic forces than Western destructive capitalism.

Chinese values, however, are distinctly opportunistic. In our book *China Calling* we provide a description of Chinese values and how they govern behavior. We show how opportunities are mixed with opportunism (self-interest seeking with guile). We also say that the Chinese door was held open with wads of cash. As *Time* magazine pointed out in March 2009, we see Hunan Valin buying 16.5 per cent of Fortescue Metals, Minmetals paying off the debt of Oz Minerals, and the Chinese government paying off a US$15 billion loan to the Russian oil company Rosneft. China, however, also met its match when Libya defended itself against any purchase of Calgary-based Verenex Energy – a company with stakes in Libya. In other words, China is not only buying, lending and pro-curing, it is also attempting strategic positions, thus making the oil-rich and ore-rich very wary of the real intentions of the Chinese. This wariness spilled over into a rejection by Australian sharehold-ers in June 2009 of Chinalco's attempts to gain further control of RTZ. A deal that looked good during the depressed commodity prices of spring 2009 looked greedy by the summer. The detention of Stern Hu, the Chinese-born Australian executive of RTZ, may be a sign that his part in the *guanxi* obligation system is under review.

The problem

China, it is noted, does not recognize stakeholders. Traditional imperialist ways continue to consider workers as paid servants – part of the household but not of its decision-making. Sharehold-ers have bought shares and are free to sell them. What long-term benefits beyond initial capital restructuring do shareholders bring? (The Chinese may have a point here; Western regulators were con-cerned about hedge-fund buying on margin for short-term share-holder ploys, but did little about it until it was too late). A jail term imposed on a Chinese executive in Singapore, for making false financial statements on the trading of jet fuel, was a preventative measure designed to reassure other shareholders. The executive, however, did no wrong in the eyes of the company stakeholder – the Chinese government. And it will happen again when Chinese state funds are at risk overseas. The communist blinker on the Confucian eye of the Chinese trader has not dimmed an ability to spot a deal in the making. But do not let that word communism fool you – Mao maintained a traditional, imperialist hierarchy. And so does the present Chinese state: it is following several millennia of centralized control.

When doing deals, Western theory argues for a control over net-worked opportunism through contract law, but also notes that, as a contract grows more complex, governance decreases. The Chinese welcome complex deals. Governance then becomes relational, a traditional network with control based on ostracism and the threat of 'losing face'. A simple deal, evidenced, for example, by bills of exchange or lading, is not a problem for the Chinese. They would prefer, however, international law for basic governance systems but with relational controls controlling opportunistic behavior whenever arrangements get complex. *Caveat regulator* – the regulatory authorities must be wary and watchful.

The Chinese use the transaction activity globally to expand relational resources when larger deals are essential. Legal advice often follows, rather than precedes, the deal. The Chinese will thus rely on arbitration procedures rather than confrontation in courts of law, but will prefer arbitration after, rather than before, action. If Chinese networks are to be understood, then the prevalence of maximizing any potential options for future deals must be accepted. The *guanxi* system does this through the creation of *renqing* (reciprocal obligations). There is a manipulative element. The uncertain, implicit nature of Chinese reciprocity is not always identifiable from the initial investment in the *guanxi* transaction. There is, therefore, the potential for breakdown. Knowing you have granted an option but not knowing its size or timing can be stressful. High levels of internal network trust case the fear.

It is therefore not a question of greed overcoming fear when the Chinese invest in a risky deal, but of greed overcoming *guanxi*. Where there is a lack of networked connections, as in the case of peasants rising up against prefectural authorities, distrustful confrontation will follow. Chinese global exchange is integrating but the system of networks is fragile. Clear consideration, with an unequivocal trust in international legal enforcement, is required to ease tensions. Relational trust depends on acceptance as partners within a network. The potential for confrontation can be lessened with mutual respect – but that takes time.

The solution

Our solution is therefore simple. It is economic exchange, the driver of trade over millennia, which is forcing change. This change is affecting basic individual values, the values derived from past national and family struggles for survival. The following characteristics, identified by researchers Haley and Tan, are common to experience-based Asian and opportunistic (particularly overseas Chinese) management:

- Hands-on experience – with a high level of senior management involvement.

- Transfer of knowledge – by conceptualizing rather than analytical skills.

- Qualitative information – externally sourced, sometimes subjective and often networked.

- Holistic information processing – more intuitive and less sequential.

- Action-driven decision making – reflecting an authoritative management

The Western penal code could not and did not prevent the leaders of organizations such as Enron, Tyco International, WorldCom, Parmalat and Refco, nor the accused pyramid schemer Bernard Madoff, from taking opportunistic advantage of shareholders and investors. The bankers, brokers and advisors are not guilt-free. Opportunism is not confined to the lower orders in mercantile trade. 'Subprime' describes financiers as well as mortgagees. Complexity in the West creates chances for the sharp operator. Opportunistic Chinese are therefore not likely to feel intimidated by complex arrangements. Indeed, the more complex a deal, the better the opportunity to imitate Western failures to enforce its terms. Hedge funds and their opacity could prove to be imitative gold mines for the Chinese financial entrepreneur.

The Chinese will therefore look for opportunities overseas where the rules are clear. The capitalist system is good at laying down rules, and the Chinese are seizing their chance. It is preferable, cash in hand, to purchase a company than to start up as a competitor. Private equity firms such as Kohlberg Kravis Roberts use extensive gearing to raise cash. The Chinese just raise cash. Their bid for RTZ in 2009 is not a convoluted geared/share swap deal but money for shares and capital for development. How old-fashioned – and sensible. But RTZ shareholders, notwithstanding a change in their company chairman and a tweak in the terms of the bid, felt they were better off without a major Chinese shareholding. Western investors need to take a hard look at their customers – the ones who actually pay the first transaction towards a dividend.

Innovation in developing an industry is amended by the Chinese to imitate and survive through merger and acquisition. It is much simpler to copy the controls already widespread in a global institution or industry than to change them in a creative fashion. Partial innovation is a result of change caused by old solutions not matching new problems. It is this process that can be called a gradual 'paradigm shift' and it depends on accepting that change is needed. The true revolution for paradigm change occurs when a totally new perspective resolves more problems in better ways. Deng Xiaoping recognized this when he started the Age of Reform in the late 1970s.

For the Chinese, their paradigm shift is towards the purchase of Western organizations rather than the more difficult innovation needed to expand their own institutions overseas. Economic expansion is allowed, military control is not, but then one is necessary to protect the other. The Chinese imitate quickly where the rules are simple. Where imitation by the Chinese is a threat, the Western opportunistic solution must be to accelerate consolidation through its own mergers or acquisitions, using size as the defensive resource. The problem is that, unlike American football, switching from large defensive teams to swift attack teams is time-consuming. The West is slow to change.

For example, the banking crisis can be put into an imitative context. Newspaper articles in 2005 discussed an investment by the Royal Bank of Scotland (RBS) in the Bank of China. It was argued that RBS must have negotiated compensation terms if the Bank of China should end up with financial problems not discernible from its published numbers. Claiming that nobody in the West can put an accurate value on a stock percentage of a Chinese state-owned bank without fooling themselves, the articles have proved to be red herrings and misdirected. The tables have been turned on the clever journalists. The British government partly nationalized RBS and, as the ultimate controlling RBS shareholder in the Bank of China, had to persuade the Chinese to end the relationship and allow RBS to sell out its share because of its own RBS toxic financial assets. The moral of the story is clear – the Chinese and everyone *knew* that their banks were in bad shape and took precautions, but the

Western governments' incompetence at regulating the Western banking and financial systems meant that the West did *not* know what was happening until too late. Which system is the worse?

The value of a relationship in China is, it must now be repeated, not purely monetary but rests in its network potential. At an interface, when negotiating or analyzing investment strategies, it is necessary to establish the information network level in advance. How much information is passed between the two parties is dependent on the levels of trust. At the network periphery, low levels of trust imply low levels of information. The West must realize that trust cannot be bought; it must be earned. Becoming trustworthy is the challenge. An investment into a network (*guanxi* connections) is one of time and of relational development. Losing relationships can be expensive in the long run.

Secreting the state

A great part of the problem arises from the limited and secretive flow of information, best suited to conglomerate internal networks. Chinese walls allow qualitatively sourced 'knowledge' to spread quickly. The prime mover instinct within Chinese management is high. Their expertise in short-term trading and their instinct to see opportunities around every corner make Chinese management believe 'intuitively' that now is the time and now is the hour. Failures result not so much from actions as from prevarications.

The way the world increasingly divides is between sources and uses, between suppliers of raw materials and processors of these commodities, between Brazil and Russia on the one hand, and India and China on the other (the 'BRIC' countries, the building blocks of a new world order). This division will become more and more apparent as the world approaches the mid-century. With the BRIC meetings in Russia during the summer of 2009, it is clear that these countries are seeking a grouping of nations to challenge Western economic dominance. China and India will be the chief controllers over finished goods and services, while Brazil and Russia will be their chief suppliers of raw materials for processing. Demographically, India has the greatest chance to grow over the period, since its working population will probably increase relative to China's in the wake of the weakening Chinese one-child policy.

Both Brazil and Russia will be overshadowed by India and China by 2050, but of rather more significance, however, are the emerging market strategies of these countries and their relative interdependence. Brazil's great resources of iron ore (for industry) and soya (for foodstuffs) will be highly prized by the other three as essential commodities. Although its growth rate is lower, its prosperity and stability are at present greater than either India's or China's, primarily because of its globally integrated economy and manufacturing potential. Russia will continue to trade on its abundant energy resources (chiefly oil and natural gas), which will mask the fall in its working population, its volatile government and its poor infrastructure, while engaging ever more closely with China to dynamize its faltering economy. China has a crucial role to play in curbing Russia's increasingly roguish, bristling and ballistic new regime by drawing off some of its more deadly firepower into more productive pursuits. India's manufacturing and services capacity, particularly in industrial and consumer goods – and especially in IT and programming – will enable it to become a major economic force to be reckoned with as China's major competitor in these areas. Within this vital nexus of interdependence, China's power to galvanize the economies of these other three countries through strategic trade and investment will be paramount.

With the demise of many financial traders, the overseas Chinese with experience in major financial centers may clear their desks and create a Chinese investment and broking house. Our first prediction is that Chinese relational networks are strong enough to set this strategy in motion – either through acquisition (we must remember that past greed used the capital markets as sources of both income and capital gain, so control is possible) or imitation. Control over one's own destiny is a primary Chinese drive – a protection against external aggression and uncertainty. Better the head of a chicken than the tail of an ox.

In China, there is a tendency to less moderation, increased opportunism, decreased mutual dependency, and changes in traditional ways. These changes must not be confused with individual destinies. The Chinese traditionally dislike teamwork, as it means working across networks and not comfortably within them. Teamwork links individuals and, traditionally, the Chinese links with each other, and with Westerners, are fraught. As middle management gain greater autonomy in flexible, flatter organizational structures, so the need for collective action becomes more important when the middle and lower management network is extended. Foreigners are increasingly part of the extended relationship.

Therefore, it is these simple alterations in Chinese relational networks which reflect the changing nature of Chinese economic strategy. The *guanxi* networks are primarily information and transaction networks. They are controls over bad behavior using ostracism as the penalty. They are supported by common collective values, reflecting the attitudes necessary to govern Chinese behavior. It is the increasingly knowledgeable and increasingly specialized network that will make the opportunistic move overseas. It may not be an organization in the Western sense, but it is a company of prime movers in an economic sense. The removals van is heading for the Western financial services and mining industry, and it is forcing a fire sale of toxic paper. The Chinese watch and wait for the final consequences of the slaughter on Wall Street and in the City of London.

We can now produce a further global prediction. Chinese expansion overseas will not be led through the legal or accountancy professions. Historically, the divergence of practices, the different rules of a global game, has just been too large for any convergence to take place in the short to medium term. The Chinese advantage, however, rests with the contractual nature of the Western professions. Subcontracting of accountancy and legal services is perfectly acceptable in the West. There is no need to imitate, merge or acquire – merely to pay the pipers to play in the counting houses and inns of court.

Imitation within China is, on the other hand, extremely likely. Copying Western legal statutes and accountancy regulations for adaptation in China enables international demands to be met. Enforcement, however, will remain relational, but the statutes will be there for external inspection. The most important concession to the West will establish *ex-post* governance of contracts through arbitration. This allows a negotiated outcome between two parties in contractual dispute to be settled – more quickly than adversarial legal combat, and more cheaply too.

We see a continual adaptation in Chinese relational opportunism. The Chinese are expanding the range of practical options in response to differences between domestic and global categories of economic exchange. Resolving new global problems provides opportunities for implementing ideas not considered previously in the decision-making process. In this way, traditional methods of implementation can be adapted, but not necessarily abandoned, in favor of the new.

Opportunism knocks

The problems emanating from quality control in Chinese manufactures are not merely seen as an internal, factory-specific problem. Cheaper outsourcing copies Western practice, but when the Western buyer forces Chinese factories down in price, the outsourcing to less expensive and less reliable local suppliers creates an imitation that goes badly wrong – only the price, but not the quality, is outsourced. The Chinese meet this issue with government-led delegations to the West, clearly signaling a relational priority level.

Change in Chinese relational management provides opportunities incorporating both Western and Chinese characteristics. Crossing a river by feeling for stepping stones (a Deng Xiaoping exhortation) makes clear the direction for success, but not the timing of a successful arrival. Patience remains a highly regarded Chinese value. For example, the larger investments by the Chinese in overseas corporations may be eclipsed by a plethora of stealth vehicles on the over the counter (OTC) and alternative investment markets (AIM). Patience here would allow an ultimate reversal by acquisition into suitable Western organizations when the timing is right, the credentials are established, and the vagaries of the market are understood. Self-interest-seeking with guile? Depends on how you perceive the behavior.

We can thus summarize modern Chinese international opportunism in three simple statements:

- The Chinese adopt a people approach and relational guidance for complex contextual issues, but a contractual, task approach and market governance for simpler, specific issues. There is a decrease in hierarchical power distance with increased heterogeneity in problem solutions, and some loosening in the traditional constraints of face and *renqing* obligations. In terms of resources, this implies a non-social commitment: run the African strip mine efficiently and then move on. There is no ethical consideration.

- The Chinese resolve ambiguity through the acceptance of different time frames for sequential or fluid transactions and activities. The Chinese will choose between either structured Western styles or fluid, more ambiguous, Chinese styles depending on the complexity and requirements of the task. In terms of financial investment, they put the cash into a deal using Western market principles, but then create shareholder control on a relational basis. This can be seen in terms of Chinese attitude to risk – they do not do full, formal financial calculations, but base their risk assessment on relational obligations for future renegotiation. The Chinese will operate where many would be lost in the analysis. Risk management attitudes in the West must alter to accommodate China's approach.

- The Chinese combine a fact-based approach with an expressive style, depending on the complexity at issue. Formality is subject to governance choices, given that communication requiring high levels of trust (for example, within a network) will remain informal and high context, but with peripheral, formal 'contractual' trust increasing. In political and diplomatic discussions, the Chinese prefer to talk first (and often) in general terms, not taking the lead, but choosing to go with the flow of the group before getting down to specifics based on their opening position.

The major problem faced by the West is in recognizing the Chinese for what they are rather than focusing purely on what they are doing. Ambiguity is essential in Chinese activities – it allows a saving of face by claiming that you were always right. It allows guile to prevail and opportunities to be taken when and where they arise. It is not two-faced, it is twofold. It is an attempt to maintain options that might in fact be mutually exclusive. It cannot be understood by using Western logic, but remains eminently sensible – keep your cards close to your chest and let others guess what you hold.

CHAPTER 3

Environment

> It is most difficult always to remember that the increase of every living being is constantly being checked by unperceived injurious agencies; and that these same unperceived agencies are amply sufficient to cause rarity, and finally extinction.
>
> (Charles Darwin, *The Origin of Species*, (1859) Ch. X – 'On Extinction')

Introduction

When we make decisions about industry or the military, or any action that involves change, we are limited in understanding the consequences. Global warming, chlorofluorocarbons (CFCs) in the atmosphere, 'collateral damage' and unexploded ordnance, chemicals, insecticides, fertilizers and such like, often have effects we do not foresee – they are unperceived injurious agencies in Darwin's encompassing sense. These human-made injuries are caused by our inability to think hard enough. We all pursue 'bounded rationality' – behavior that is meant to be rational and thoughtful, but suffers from limitations caused by factors such as lack of knowledge, foresight, skill and time. Looking for the sharpest needle in the sewing box is not as rational as producing any needle sharp enough to sew with. The timely solution is 'satisficed'. When confronted with a number of variables, 'satisficing' is a bounded but rational act. In trying to move beyond those bounds, Al Gore, the Nobel Laureate, notes that the human species is facing a global emergency endangering the planet. Darwin would agree.

But why not act faster? Recent research identifies three factors as major controls over decision-making. First, uncertainty, and its impact on bounded rationality, remains a prime factor. Second, personal emotion, stemming from the individual, affects the decision. Third, the social context in which the individual acts is also an inescapable control. In particular, personal experience and the social context will both control behavior and inhibit deviation from the group norm. In globalization, two simple control variables compete in the same space – the domestic way of doing things can clash with the international way. Criteria governing conflicting rules, and different ways of doing things, cause the dynamic system to break down. Global warming is not an immediate personal experience, and the social context for the West is certainly not 'green'. The failure of Kyoto and the internal arguing while the planet dies is a Western loss, in particular the attitude of the USA under President Bush. Fiddling while Rome burns is as nothing compared to American denials while the earth drowns as the seas rise.

But China is trying. To understand China, to see its real environmental values, you must see conditions down on the farm in rural China. You can make your way to the Ming hideaway of Cuandixia, an ancient hive of dwellings as close-packed as the bees that swarm around it, clinging to the side of a mountain some sixty miles north-west of the capital, Beijing. The little settlement has been the extended living space of the local Han family over many generations. The villagers scrape a very modest living from offering overnight stays to visitors from Beijing. The sleeping quarters are cool interiors with rolls of foam rubber laid over trestle tables. The food they offer is their own supper: tasty herb omelettes, savory pancakes, tofu and ground corn-cob soup. The Chinese desire for a healthy environment is rooted in their recent, non-industrialized past.

The problem

Two main areas may help China to deal with its environmental affairs; education, and science and technology. The more Europe and China understand each other, the better it will be for both economic growth, and for environmental and societal protection. Policy dilemmas in these areas are faced most starkly in China, where it is often assumed that the former can only be achieved at the expense of the latter. Because we need both, there is no real contradiction. Rather, China needs help to promote energy-saving methods, to ensure efficient growth and to incentivize the use of energy-saving transport in its infrastructure development, and in seeking the golden mean of balanced growth for the coming days of disastrous global warming, subsequent droughts and seasonal disruptions of crops. The West may hope for the best, but deep down it hopes that China succeeds where the West has failed. The real fear is if China fails.

At the present time, however, it is the lack of trust shown by the West to China that creates a major problem. Environmental control in China is low and Western greed forces the Chinese into short cuts. Metallic lead in toys sourced by Mattel, and breaking plastic bottle caps sourced by Wal-Mart, are just a couple of instances. With China previously supplying a good 40 per cent of global products there is an increasing focus on China as the bad guy. But political democratic tricks in the West are decreasing the trust levels. A Chinese factory manager commits suicide and the West still shakes its fist. How many Western executives would fall on their sword for their errors? Many are paid off with lucrative pensions yet their financial products have caused more global damage than have low-quality painted toys.

Such incongruities affect Chinese behavior. The West points to defending the planet and its environment, but is slow to act itself and quick to point at China as an accident waiting to happen. The vast majority of Chinese may be in the economic pyramid but they inhabit its base. Their aspirations and expectations are being heightened by the color television in the corner of every family home. Pyramids are inherently stable if the base is undisturbed. The apex may hold the power, but the view from the bottom, of fairness in that power, is less and less distinct. Increased overseas focus, tighter controls over pollution, taxing corruption where penalties are difficult, harmony rather than horse trading, and many other less black and white stances on the domestic front all serve to ease the likelihood that the people will call the mandate of Party power to account. Yet global greed creates domestic envy and advances corruption.

No matter how purposefully China might move towards a true comity of nations, if the country cannot bring under control and rid itself of its two most crippling scourges – both human-made and both rampantly expanding – it will not prevail. First, it must address the internal, private pollution of TB, HIV/AIDS, syphilis and other sexually transmitted diseases that have become a serious affliction for its migrant, floating populations. Second, the full extent of its external, public despoiling of the environment must be tackled. There can be no other course, or its population fails.

A further blight on progress is the widespread counterfeiting of other countries' proprietary branded products, euphemistically, but elegantly, known as the infringement of intellectual property rights. This makes Chinese entrepreneurs seem more like Raffles, the jewel thief, than the dishonest merchants they really are. While imitation is always flattering, it is only ingenious innovation that will carry China forward. Yet many poor workers in China find the West's pricing of intellect an unfair burden set well above the cost of manufacture. The patent protection afforded to life-saving drugs may be seen by many of the world's poor as a trick to kill them off while manufacturers get richer.

The severe acute respiratory syndrome (SARS) crisis several years ago highlighted how gravely at risk China was of suffering a major pandemic. Up to that point, government policy had been not to admit or simply to cover up such outbreaks of infectious diseases and to treat them as a state secret. The later bird flu outbreaks also showed a reluctance to share crucial information on the spread of the infection with a wider world. The government failed to provide the requested avian samples to the World Health Organization (WHO) and to the international community, and insisted on developing its own vaccines. The ingrained sense of secrecy and shame over the issue is pervasive and will recur should swine flu prove to become more deadly than a straightforward viral pandemic. China's strict border controls will seek to keep the virus out, rather than in.

The solution

In the matter of HIV and AIDS, the authorities do realize the full extent of the problem and are tackling it on a broad front. However, a major part of these measures involve simply jailing infected drug addicts and sex workers. The epidemic has not yet reached African levels, and those infected do receive free anti-retroviral treatment, but medical monitoring remains haphazard and is at best based on guesswork. Blood donation has been a major transmission vector of the disease, through infected needles. Those likely to be infected are not routinely tested for HIV, yet xenophobia dictates that those returning from overseas will be! Blood plasma has been pooled and then corruptly used for random transfusions, with inevitable dire consequences. Another corruption scandal has involved the supply of adulterated milk powder for infants, damaging the organs of many and killing a few. In China, with the one-child policy and enforced sterilization, deaths of the young are particularly devastating.

The Party is aware of the extreme difficulty that many Chinese encounter in obtaining medical treatment. There is no effective medical insurance system in place to enable people to meet the expense of any treatment or operation beyond routine clinic visits. Life-threatening illnesses and accidents can only be treated if patients and victims can borrow enough money to meet the costs – and this often brings crippling indebtedness. By far the most common affliction is hepatitis B, which has become almost endemic among the Chinese. Infants are generally vaccinated against the most common diseases, but there are still large gaps in the provision and availability of treatment, in most cases because of the sheer distance from medical care, and lack of money. The recession again offers a potential solution. The masses will not remain as quiet as the silent factories. A social rather than an economic push is now being proposed by the Party, with medical care being more freely available. Health rather than wealth!

Air pollution still remains a problem, especially in Beijing, but also in all the major and minor cities and towns in the country. There are two main root causes of the problem that have straightforward solutions. First, the old Chinese refrain that 'the mountains are high and the emperor is far away' portrays a ground-level lack of concern, and second, economic growth has been given pride of place above all else. The Party is beginning to regain ground in controlling the provinces and in its attempts to create an orderly civil society and environment, but it cannot wait much longer until environmental protection measures are properly affordable. Further delay will build into a dangerous catalyst for unrest in the country.

There are countryside protests over polluted rivers. Factory effluents have caused workers to smash up plant and machinery. Fish,
a major source of protein for many inland town and city folk, are
poisoned and dying, and the government has responded with a
'green GDP' campaign initiative, a curiously ineffectual palliative,
which papers over the problems by doling out energy efficiency
targets – almost all of which it fails to meet. Another old refrain is
sounded, '*Shang mian you zheng ce, xia lu you dui ce*': 'There are
policies from above, but ways of dealing with them from below'.
Grass-roots action is therefore not unusual in China – hence the
authorities' fear of any uncontrolled rebellion.

This environmental degradation provokes widespread local activ-
ism. International groups such as the World Wildlife Fund (WWF)
and Greenpeace operate in China, but often as registered businesses rather than as non-governmental organizations (NGOs),
which heightens local suspicion of further meddling by foreigners.
Forceful direct measures taken by activists invariably lead to their
being jailed. Courage comes at a heavy price: detention and physical restraint are used to quash dissent. And all the while, that vital
balance in the country is poised precariously along the rich/poor
divide, buffeted in the struggle between reformers and conserva-
tives in the Party. People were dragged headlong by a belief in the
thrust for prosperity at all costs, but are now focusing on health.

The prospect of continuing environmental degradation while serving the global consumer is unacceptable. The cash surplus of China
is shifting overseas, regionally into Vietnam and Cambodia, and
further afield into Africa and South America. The Chinese will
import expertise to clean up the mess and export purchasing power
to pollute somewhere else. Others' backyards are fair game – they
have no *guanxi* connections. Over the mid- to long term, China is
looking to meet domestic demand as a priority. Two-thirds of its
people largely miss out on the benefits of the current boom. Social
welfare is a priority to avoid disaffection and destabilizing social
unrest in the inland and nether provincial regions of the country.
The levels of medical facilities and social security systems for
basic health, welfare and employment will need to be raised swiftly
to meet the clamor for equal treatment from the many millions who
feel marginalized and dispossessed. Larger farming communities
will be created and developed into effective economic units, and

the fall-out of employees from the former state-owned enterprises will need to be taken up in redeployment into jobs in other new industries to be established in Central and Western China, well away from the coastal conurbations of the Eastern seaboard.

Along with all of this, the cost of massive clean-ups of environmental degradation (already a catalyst for widespread organized protests) and of corruption – held in place by officials' threats of mutual whistle-blowing – will need to be addressed urgently as a budgetary priority. The West has a tremendous opportunity to offset its consumer purchases by 'bartering' its clean up and waste management expertise. In Taiwan, the influx of foreign expertise in this area during the late 1980s and early 1990s was welcomed. Trading part of China's surplus for a cleaner environment is a safe political step.

Meanwhile the process of beautifying Beijing continues apace, with the planting of floral banks and painting of the more decrepit façades of *hutongs* or back lanes and alleys in a standard swash of grey, rendering them curiously invisible, like unobtrusive stage flats. One *hutong* house has a notice taped to its door: 'Please do not bother us. These are ordinary living quarters'. Such is the concern for the preservation of these single-storey, semi-slum dwellings with their secluded inner courtyards that visitors take an almost prurient interest in prying into them to make sure that they are still intact.

Property values were driven to ridiculous heights by the 2008 Olympic hoopla and have duly ridden to a fall; but there has also been intensive new investment in huge, new airport terminals and new subway lines, and now in a massive infrastructure programme of bridges and roads to stretch the country's transport network. However, the real challenge for the government to meet is slowly to slake the ravenous hunger and thirst for jobs and knowledge of the 700 million *lao baixing* – the 'Old Hundred Names' peasant farmers in the countryside. If the Party fails to hasten environmental progress there, it will surely struggle.

One of the biggest barriers to predicting where China is going is the Western belief in an order to things – not so much a belief in the paradigmatic continuation of physical laws, but a belief that society must be ordered by imposing societal law. The Chinese do not think in that way. The concept that laws are for the guidance of wise men but the obedience of fools is an excuse for disobedience mirrored in the Chinese *nan de hu tu* (hard to translate, but basically meaning that wisdom and foolishness can be interchangeable).

And that is perhaps why economists shelter behind discontinuities. They are unexpected and unpredictable, and are factored out of most calculations. This is the real environmental problem. Economics is a subject dear to the Chinese (and to many in the West) because it allows a semblance of science to creep into government decision-making. Politicians therefore tend to panic when economists do not predict discontinuities or know exactly how to deal with them. The environment and global warming is a massive discontinuity, which global economists should relish. For once there is an opportunity to link basic economic behavior with real geo-sciences. But no, back the West goes to stimulus packages and defence of the global car and oil industries. Opportunity lost.

The disaster

In modern China, the use of mobile phones is extensive and increasing. A small panic, normally contained in recent years, could now cause a calamity through instant communications, which would be quite disastrous. Chinese rumors spread quickly. Our final prediction is that an accident of an environmental nature will create that panic. Not so much a geological earthquake as a chemical or biological catastrophe. The pell-mell drive for economic prosperity is a drive designed to keep the population under control, but not driven to poisoned rivers and fields. Energy and infrastructure failures will frustrate many. Inflation in foodstuffs is now coming down from previously high peaks. The old emperor's mandate allowed the population to overturn the emperor if he failed them. No need for spoiling ballot papers, no need to vote them out nicely; the Chinese have a stronger, traditional hold on the politicians' promises of 'a chicken in every pot'. They are entitled to another revolution. We read an unsavoury environmental one in the dynamic runes.

This is a problem created as a result of the jobless masses. While adding modern agricultural processes to farming methods is positive, what will the farmers' families do with mechanization? There are not enough colleges for the future mechanics, engineers and agricultural specialists. There are no more jobs on building sites or in factories. Increasingly, this 'new problem' for China uncovers the dynamic forces that open borders stimulate. Controls over opportunism, resources and investments are changing from the traditional ways of doing things. But they are not aligned, and struggle to balance demand, supply and direction. The potential for a bursting of societal and environmental dams of despondency is high.

Stripping the Earth's resources merely to serve present market demand is not a long-term solution. Problem-solving using Chinese systemic controls will help to check Western consumer sprees. In Chinese tradition, if it isn't broken, by all means adapt it – but don't replace it. The West, in a mirror image and reflective mode, must emphasize relational and reciprocal structures when globalizing. The West should reduce the clamor for open market economies and look for societal, group solutions. So far, the West and East are found wanting, with economists having more say than warranted by their 'dismal science'. Indeed, modern economics is almost religious in its defence of its base assumptions – and, like religion, it is only the interpretation of events that matters. The environmentalists must move much more quickly, more forcefully and more scientifically in asserting their claims to saving the world.

CHAPTER 4

Might

Let us have faith that right makes might, and in that faith, let us, to the end, dare to do our duty, as we understand it.

(Abraham Lincoln, *Cooper Union Address*,
New York, February 27, 1860)

Introduction

Faith in our own national values dictates our cultural behavior, which in turn dictates our decision-making. A sense of duty and traditional ways of doing things are part of the same dynamic. Faith provides a theoretical belief when dealing with a new and unknown future. It may be vague, it may result in a plan, but rests, quite simply, on its premises that right makes might. Past practice, often subject to national regulations and institutional influences, shows the way in which thinking is done in the face of past uncertainty – the outcome of successful past actions. Our premise now is that might is the power behind Chinese military thinking, under their belief that China is right.

The Chinese thinking system can best be illustrated by invoking Sun Tzu and his *The Art of War*, a popular handbook in the West. His strategic advice on generalship and the waging of battle is primarily opportunistic, excellent for winning skirmishes and temporary advantage, but not for sustaining the effort needed to maintain a real, long-term presence in alien territory.

China depends on opportunism at the periphery, a tactical activity. A long-term strategy should be flexible and sustainable, with the retention of any advantage being more important than the immediate gain. Modern Chinese strategy aims to colonize by creating and taking opportunities, with Western techniques being used for the colonization and Chinese tactics deployed for the battles. Chinese expansion has different but compatible rules for the short-term (battle) and long-term (colonization) time requirements.

And here lies China's strength. From a specific national perspective, national cultures provide an interesting contrast between West, East and Africa. The point to ponder is the positioning of China. The Middle Kingdom is central to the developed and developing nations; it appears better placed to straddle global power bases than is the West. Indeed, China's advances in Africa are aided and abetted by the West's focus on post-colonial, interest-bearing aid – but with conditions. Chinese assistance is not more altruistic, but is less confrontational. China looks to capture resources at the lowest cost while keeping options open and unspecified – basically an Asian hire purchase scheme.

The problem

Chinese history constantly shifted between the power battles of mighty forces. The fall of the imperial Qing Dynasty with the October revolution of 1911 did away with the emperor but also with the mandarins, the scholar–official class of administrators and magistrates who ruled China in the emperor's name. With the cutting off of their pigtails, ordinary Chinese men symbolically dropped their deference to this highly centralized authority and its command to 'tremble and obey' in the face of the emperor's representative. The new republic let chaos loose in the land. Acknowledged as the founder of modern China, Sun Yat-sen did not trust his fellows and set up a government system allowing a cross-check of performance at the ministerial level. Such a cross-check can and does prevent normal administrative action from taking place when it cows officials into avoiding potential challenge and subsequent penalties. Chinese government officials still keep their heads down lest the cross-check turn into cross-fire. It is ministerial protection at the highest level.

But the new empire fell prey to competing warlords. The nationalist government and its attendant political party were formed in the early part of the twentieth century. The Second World War

provided an opportunity for communism in the form of Maoist totalitarianism and warlord imperialism to gain a disguised
foothold. Subsequent fighting resulted in the flight of Chiang
Kai-shek and nationalist leaders to Taiwan, taking many of the
treasures of China with them. General Chiang and his national
party, began Kuomintang (KMT) rule in Taiwan by shooting
several thousand locals in the southern port town of Kaohsiung.
If anyone wonders why there is indigenous distrust of the KMT
party in the Taiwanese elections, it is because it is as historical
as Irish distrust of English rule. The Kaohsiung 'tea party' was
bloodily put down.

Although Chiang Kai-shek was Sun's heir apparent, he received
not the mantle and mandate of power, but rejection from the mass
of the Chinese people. Nevertheless, Sun is firmly acknowledged
as the godfather of both the communist and the nationalist revolutions, each still competing for moral supremacy in China. His
name is revered, as the revisionism of the post-Mao era makes
plain. Sun – a Christian, son of émigré sugar planters from Hawaii,
sent to study medicine in Hong Kong – dared to foment debate in
Guangdong. He was the living embodiment of Chinese hopes of
redress from the West for all the indignities and wrongs inflicted
under the corrupt mandarins. But he was shouldered ruthlessly
aside in the immense power vacuum which followed their fall. He
was never allowed to attempt that greatest feat of all: to align China
(the Middle Kingdom) in equal partnership with other sovereign
peoples of the Earth – an alignment that is now economic and soon
to be military in its motion.

For the People's Republic of China, therefore, the potential for a
non-military reunification with the Republic of China on Taiwan is
probably more likely to be secured through the KMT politicians.
Both the mainland People's Party and the Taiwanese KMT believe
in one China. The problem is that neither rules all of China. Reconciliation through economic and political means is obviously preferable to military action. But strategies are forever opportunistic and
options are never closed. The military build up by China is one of
resource heterogeneity. Submarines to sink Taiwan? Or to prevent
US pressure on shipping lanes through the Malacca Straits? Western actions in the Middle East are being imitated and adapted by
China in Asia.

Basically, overseas democracy is getting in the way of Asian harmony. In parts of China – especially around the old nationalist strongholds of Chongqing and Kunming – nationalist sympathizers retain some allegiance. The opportunity for any future democracy in China could well result in KMT opposition. The tolerance of such an opposition would be enhanced if the KMT could bring Taiwan into the fold. Taiwanese calls for independence are primarily calls for recognition, heard but unheeded by the rest of the world. Economic exchange is, however, allowing the Taiwanese to invade the mainland. During the Tiananmen demonstrations and subsequent dystopian response in the late 1980s, American Nike representatives who had fled China to Hong Kong were asked, on the CNN news channel, what was happening to their factories. Their reply was simply that they were presently being run by their Taiwanese managers.

Twenty years later, considerable individual Taiwanese investment and expertise are an intrinsic part of modern entrepreneurial wealth in China, thus weakening past levels of mutual suspicion. Economic activity is part of the Chinese character and will prove to be a large part of the answer to the problem of reconciliation. If a broker is required in negotiations, the greater understanding of Western ways is currently found among the Taiwanese. What therefore matters now is the integrity of the Chinese empire and control of its boundaries, from the Russian rivers of the North to the high mountain passes of the Himalayas in the South. North Korea and Vietnam remain virtual buffer states. Any slackness at the soft end of the border with Central Asia is tautened with oil deals and technology and the bracing presence of the People's Liberation Army (PLA) and their growing Navy. No point in being right if the might is missing.

The solution

The Chinese have suffered the repeated ministrations of meddlesome officials controlling their work, their movements, and even the size of their family. Modernization at a government level is tough and must be recognized as slow and cumbersome. Unlike the European Commission, where the audit service merely notes that the books cannot be balanced, the Chinese system seeks to balance issues in a modern, focused but flexible fashion.

The Chinese have the monetary and military might to order a significant portion of the world's affairs. What they do not yet have is sufficient affiliation to, and authoritative interface with, the councils of the world and their norms of governance to be a stable element in international relations. Facts are all encumbered with myth, legend and apocryphal stories. What we do know now is the nature of this race. We know its historic habitat, its suffering and its defense of its own ground. Caged and corralled in their own particular sphere for millennia, the Chinese are coming out as battalions under a chain of command as swift and secure as that of the Catholic Church. It is China that will assert its hegemony over East and Central Asia. Any Western kowtowing to Chinese might is now seen as a weakness in the East.

The northern borders are coming down, with Japan commencing 'ice-breaking' trips to China, and China reciprocating with 'ice-thawing' return visits. The North Korean nuclear and rocket crises have improved China's power base and weakened that of its neighbors and of the USA. China's political demands at the time of writing consist of a strategic play aimed at restructuring its external borders. Now Hong Kong and Macau, next Taiwan, then the Koreas, followed by non-Muslim South-East Asia. The West must now properly understand modern China's might, and play its part in China's development of regional security alliances that prepare for compromise and the prevention of future conflict.

To understand China requires three major shifts in previous Western perspectives. First, the Confucian principle of hierarchical leadership, the ruler/subject mandate, permits a leader – and China has a history of cruel warlords as well as wise ones – to be followed relatively unquestioned. Second, the family protects itself and its members through *guanxi*. Having gained power, Mao set about breaking down the *guanxi* (of the landlord class, in particular) as a necessary step to ensure a divide-and-control governing structure. Mao targeted the family, breaking it up by forced deportation from the cities and by turning son against father and brother against brother. The nature of the *guanxi* networks in China is very strong and fundamental to the collectivist society, so the continuing use of *guanxi* networks for economic survival is unsurprising in Chinese society. It is seen as a necessary and continuing prophylactic against the might of domestic oppression and global economic misery.

Finally, the largest network in China is the PLA. Armies are more often than not civilians in uniform at a time of national emergency. Members of a standing, regular army are normally far fewer in number. A legacy from Maoist rule, the PLA in China is different. It is the nation's task force, combat-ready in the event of war, but otherwise engaged in the pursuit of commerce, the most common means of human survival. So it has always been in China. A peacetime army is put to work in great enterprises of national reconstruction – not just highways and harbors, but in gargantuan undertakings such as the Three Gorges dam on the Yangtze River, where the scale is awesome. The earthquake in Sichuan in 2008 saw the PLA mobilized as a task force for disaster relief on a vast scale.

Ultimately, any strategy using the might of a nation must still deal with political, industrial and military controls. A focus on strategy at the working level of the Chinese has been neglected in the past. Too often, strategy has concentrated on leadership and views from the top. We recommend that Chinese expansionary strategy be viewed as dependent on a wider set of governing criteria, a set containing both Western and Eastern characteristics, en route to its approximate state of unstable equilibrium. What is unclear is what relationship exists, or will exist, between social contexts of the workers and political contexts of the Party. We believe that they are intertwined and inseparable. We argue that future uncertainty is increasing as the Party realizes it must deal more with social unrest and less with economic growth. The former is fuzzy and the latter long-term.

China's borders are social defenses from India, China's main neighbor to the south, with the two countries separated by the vast natural buffer of the Himalayas. It appears that India holds a number of aces sufficient to trump China as a serious contender for supremacy in the region. These aces include, on the face of it, a more highly skilled workforce and a linguistic, democratic and educational legacy from the British Raj, equipping its citizens with a high standard of legal and commercial understanding. In addition, the government has actively promoted free enterprise and entrepreneurial activities. There is a traditional upper caste of merchants (ranking with priests and warriors) in India and no stigma attached to trade.

But set against these advantages, China is unfettered by lower-caste mobility ceilings and can offer an undoubtedly greater racial (and non-religious) homogeneity, with higher growth rates and a rather better infrastructure. In addition, the contribution of overseas Chinese to the national economy is markedly more significant than that of overseas Indians (unless Mittal Steel, Tata or the struggling Cobra beer brand prove us wrong).

Moreover, it is clear that China's overseas expansion is to forge strong alliances with potential competitors in the larger emerging economies such as Brazil, Turkey and Central Asia, in order to maintain its commercial influence and competitive advantage. The Chinese are also arriving in Eastern Europe and the European Union. Chinese links with Iran and the sheikdoms of the Middle East are increasing. The West has lost its grip there. Israel is now seen by China as a rogue state of the USA (or on democratic life-support primarily to serve as a vote gatherer in US elections).

There is an increasing economic and political power base being made available for China – with India as its nearest neighbor. It is India that threatens China, and China that threatens India: the elephant versus the dragon. The USA and Europe are customers, but China and India are competitors. The Indian push for global recognition is playing on the Chinese psyche. Recent concerns among Chinese businesses in Beijing are less about the rising renminbi and more about the power of the rupee. A race for resources by half the planet's population is a threat to economic and environmental stability. Overseas alliances by China will arise from defensive and offensive strategies. The West may watch and wonder, but the economic hegemony created by Chinese strategic relationships and financial reciprocity will result in a powerful global imperialism. The Chinese are more likely to take chances and circumvent Western best practice. There is no best practice for resource-rich Africa or the borderlands of Tibet. China cannot be blamed for tackling them in their own way.

Technological might

The Chinese have no desire to assert global domination in the software market, but neither do they wish to be subservient to calculating

American power. China recognizes that there are opportunities in adaptation. Linux is open software, supported by experts who are tired of seeing the dominance of Microsoft. Linux is also much less vulnerable to hacking attacks. Its development, from a small beginning in Sweden, has come through layer upon layer of additions and refinements by software experts and IT addicts.

The Chinese government has decided that Linux can be Sinographed or turned into a domestic software system. This adaptation, by creating specifically Chinese programming, will allow a China-only version of Linux to be deployed across Chinese governmental (civil and military) establishments, followed by businesses whenever the customs and revenue services demand its use for filing purposes. American dominance in hardware development and manufacture will lose out to the Asian entrepreneur. Soon the software systems in Asia will be Asian competitive, but also Asian compatible; not a bamboo curtain but a bamboo firewall.

It is the West that has a need of firewalls. A Toronto-based investigative organization reckons that Chinese hackers (based in Hainan Island) have succeeded in accessing Western governments and organizations. These cybercrimes, it is alleged, are in fact practice for future Chinese control of the internet and a potential threat to Western technological systems. From a Chinese perspective it is preferable to have the key to a Western door but to keep a bolt on your own. Not so much a threat as a negotiating tool.

There is clearly a great challenge to industries worldwide from Chinese technological advances. China has the capacity to produce lower-cost innovations in areas such as energy, transport and communications. It will become a magnet for research and development activities by many who can supply the necessary cultural software for China's innovative hardware. To boost its naval power, for example, new aircraft carriers are in hand. In spite of taking out one of its own space satellites in 2007 as target practice for its new range of ballistic missiles, the Chinese government vehemently discounts any intention to engage in an arms race in space (and vigorously denies any thoughts of knocking out US spy satellites, yet talks of putting a man on the moon by 2020). China has demonstrated that its navy is now a real threat, both above and under the sea.

Their ability to fire an oblique warning shot across the bows of the US Seventh Fleet in the Pacific shows clearly enough that they have no desire to be at the mercy of US forces. It seems that the real ghost in the machinery of the Chinese economy is neither the Party nor the PLA, but quite simply protectionism. China still reserves for itself the following key industries: armaments; power generation and distribution; oil and petrochemicals; telecommunications; coal; aviation; and shipping. In addition, machinery and car manufacture, IT, construction, iron and steel, and non-ferrous metals will remain under the watchful eye of the state-owned enterprises. Banking licences are on a preferential basis. The building of naval bases in Sri Lanka, in Pakistan and in South-East Asia, is a device towards Chinese protective security and not a step to invasion.

This military and economic protectionism is entrenched nationalization on a macro scale. It allows very limited room for maneuver by the private sector – let alone foreign investors – in the development of technological innovation in the economy, except in areas such as textiles, fashion, retail and tourism. However, the potential for China to produce world-class research is likely to be realized before 2020. Its universities and research centers are well endowed and release a growing stream of engineers and scientists intellectually equipped to handle innovation and technology. This will be acquired as often as it is developed in-house.

To steal a march on the West, China will rapidly develop its capacity to originate, innovate and invest in technologies for new product development. Key high-tech areas are fiber optics, semiconductors and chips for the electronics and communication and security/surveillance industries. Major advances have already been made in mobile TV chips and digital recognition scanners (for reading facial bone structure). Innofidel claims the capacity to transform mobile handsets into micro-TVs, and their scanners set in front doors will enable people to do away with house keys. But these are still minor breakthroughs in an era of highly sophisticated disruptive technologies that threaten the continuity of many international product lines.

The global knowledge and expertise gained by the overseas Chinese counter the US and other major Western countries' protection of their high-tech proprietary rights. There is a real fear of their products being copied and reproduced by China to undercut Western sales, markets and military uses. Rather than stealing or gaining foreign proprietary knowledge by industrial espionage, China has to produce its own home-grown innovations in order to compete in world markets. The scientists and engineers, graduating every year from its universities and colleges of technology, are beginning to catch up with the levels of knowledge and teaching achieved at the Massachusetts Institute of Technology (MIT) or Imperial College, London. But the much more likely route for China to take to attain any kind of parity with the West is via acquisition.

China's forward technological and industrial offensive into many areas of the wider world is like a reprise of the fabled Star Raft adventure of Admiral Cheng Ho to Africa in the fifteenth century. This time, however, there are advance bases and plentiful supply lines in place. Government agencies are arranging and providing premises and warehouses as bridgeheads into overseas markets, and a permanent support network of diplomatic, banking, customs, tax and insurance assistance to Chinese investors in overseas industries. This is also designed to expedite intelligence-gathering worldwide.

In South-East Asia, China is hungry for acquisitions to satisfy its voracious appetite for oil, gas and timber. This hunt is state-driven, and Chinese companies are not always sensitive to local anti-Chinese sentiment in the societies of Indonesia, Malaysia, Singapore and Vietnam, where they may be regarded as nouveaux riches interlopers with little understanding of local history and culture. The potential for environmental damage is very high in these regions, and dangerous flashpoints may be brewing, allowing China to flex its muscles in the face of these antipathies.

In Central Asia, China is buying up oilfields in Uzbekistan, Kazakhstan and Turkmenistan to secure its energy needs. It has forged a close alliance with Iran for a further supply of oil, chiefly for military purposes. This incursion into the former Soviet sphere of influence has naturally disquieted and upset the Russians. But it has also forged military alliances and co-operative exercises with the old Soviet vassal states, allowing Russia and China to maintain a wary strategic relationship under the Shanghai Cooperation Organization.

Russia, China's nearest neighbor and former mentor, is engaging in a volume of bilateral trade that is increasing at a rate of nearly 40 per cent a year. The two countries are bound by the import–export of machinery, high-tech products and construction materials, and have agreed to collaborate on technological innovation in energy, transport, biotechnology and infrastructure development.

In Europe, China is following the route taken by Japan and Korea – building factories and providing jobs. Made in Europe has a better brand ring than Made in China, but does mean that a future Chinese product with a Made in Europe branding can also be classified as Owned in China. It is expanding globally via the acquisition of local companies, buying up plant and technology with the added advantage of shipping facilities and operations to China if they are no longer profitable overseas. This type of asset strip is a fine capitalist ploy, learned and adapted by the Chinese.

In Africa, China is driven ever more keenly by the need to take all available oil (from Nigeria and Sudan), copper (from Namibia), metals (from Zambia), iron ore (from Mozambique), diamonds (from South Africa), timber (from Cameroon) and even cinnamon (from the Seychelles). It has played fast and loose with local leaders, dictators and warlords, providing wholesale financial and technical assistance in exchange for these vital commodities. It has, however, fallen foul of some regimes, where its arrival has brought no 'trickle down' benefit to the local economy. Typically, its own laborers are flown in to complete projects, causing great resentment among the locals. In Ethiopia, Chinese workers have been shot by rebels; and at a copper mine in Zambia, local workers went on strike, Chinese foremen have been known to fire at workers. All these incidents act as lightning rods for international opinion, but also serve to sensitize Chinese to the tensions and difficulties of expansion across cultural boundaries. China derives around 25 per cent of its energy needs from Africa at the time of writing, and its direct investment in the continent rose from US$5 million in 1991 to over US$70 billion in 2008.

In the Middle East, China already has a well-established presence through Chinamex (China Machinery and Electronics Products Exhibition Centre), based in Dubai. This serves as a major trade platform for Chinese incursions into the Gulf States and the surrounding countries in North Africa and Eastern Europe. These markets have a growing appetite for Chinese products, chiefly light industrial, agricultural and food machinery and equipment, petroleum and natural gas equipment, textiles, refrigeration and medical equipment, and hi-fi and video equipment. The 'Dragon Mart' in Dubai, at over one kilometer in length, is the largest permanent international showcase for Chinese merchandise.

In the USA, there have already been cases of Chinese approaches to control oil companies, such as Unocal, being rebuffed – a prime example of US protectionism and fear of ceding any energy resources to China. Sinopec, the state oil behemoth, and the China National Offshore Oil Corporation (CNOOC), the offshore exploration company, will not give up easily and will continue to press their claims to tap into existing conduits for energy, as demand rises in China at a rate of over 10 per cent a year.

South America is probably the most resource-rich continent and another prime target for China's insatiable hunger for control over the commodities needed to power its growth – copper from Chile, oil from Venezuela, soya from Brazil. President Chavez of Venezuela is clearly inclined to be accommodating to China, and has received US$700 million in credits from China, while Cuba is working with Sinopec on offshore oil exploration. Latin America is to receive at least US$200 billion in Chinese investment over the next few years. This is the pattern of Chinese political power emerging everywhere, as a champion of the developing world and of Third-World solidarity.

In Australia, there is an ongoing search for acquisitions in the mineral ore companies, with Australia raising its defenses and claiming that holes dug in Australian ground must remain Australian (a 'digger' we must remember is an old term for an Aussie miner – the defence is cultural as well as economic). In New Zealand, there are ongoing discussions with indigenous Maori landowning trust groups, the Chinese seeking agreements to lease forestry, farming and fishing rights.

China will need to guard against a growing perception that its initiatives, of asset purchases through financial markets in developed countries and of direct resource investment in many poorer Third-World countries, are simply a new form of colonialism. Its policy of studied non-engagement with local matters (in a long tradition of self-sufficiency and self-regulation) will run the risk of being compromised unless some of these matters (such as employment and environmental concerns) are not addressed squarely. By using their relational techniques, rather than contractual ones, the Chinese are at present able to cloud the issues and to hide the extent of their control. For Africa, and particularly for Sudan, it is now the West, colonial epaulettes replaced by chips on the shoulder, that dares to accuse China of a failure to pursue human rights in Africa.

The mighty plan

The cultural plan to advance Chinese interests on a broad front overseas has three main planks. First, they are setting up a network of branches of the 'Confucius Institute' (a centre for Chinese language teaching and sponsorship of cultural events), attached for the most part to universities, as a catalyst to further mutual reciprocity. There are more Chinese studying English in China than there are native English speakers in the world. Perhaps a little understanding from the West in the Mandarin department could do wonders in meeting China's transition on to the world stage. Second, China has only recently embraced competitive sport in several disciplines, such as soccer, rugby and athletics, where it previously had no experience or tradition beyond acrobatics, gymnastics, table tennis and badminton, and it wants to do more. Third, the associations of returned students from the USA and Europe will serve to maintain and strengthen global links, and facilitate access and collaboration with foreign and Chinese research institutions. Knowledge then becomes a relational commodity. Knowledge becomes power, and the right knowledge becomes mighty powerful.

CHAPTER 5

Society

Any society that would give up a little liberty to gain a little security will deserve neither and lose both.
(Attributed to Benjamin Franklin, eighteenth-century US statesman)

Introduction

Within Greater China, individual rights remain subsumed to Chinese values – values with strict deference to hierarchy. Hong Kong's administration was to be governed, according to its first Beijing appointed chief executive, Tung Chee-hwa, by Chinese values: 'trust, love and respect for our family and our elders; integrity, honesty and loyalty to all; commitment to education; a belief in order and stability; a preference for consultation rather than confrontation'. As an optional extra, he also mentioned 'a preference for obligation rather than individual rights'.

The small point C. H. Tung mentioned as an aside, that 'preference for obligation rather than individual rights', is the most pivotal point of all. Chinese people live constantly as part of their extended family, back and forward over time. They advance into the future facing backward, honoring their ancestors, and exacting obedience from their children. A Chinese 'obligation' means an unquestioning and unflinching devotion to family welfare and interests, and by extension to the greater family of the nation. It is almost as if, by pulling on one loose thread of individualism, the entire relational fabric of society would unravel. In such a context, dare one equate 'individual rights' with 'human rights'?

This aspect of society is constantly revisited by the Party. The Party Congress argues that rights and obligations are subjugated to the stability of society. President Hu Jintao was reported by *Xinhua* news agency on March 10, 2009 as wishing to ensure lasting peace and stability in Tibetan society by building 'a unified, democratic, prosperous and harmonious socialistic new Tibet'. Liberty is not mentioned.

The problem

What is there in Chinese society that seeks harmony but not liberty? Is liberty an individualistic concept, but harmony a communal need? From an alternative viewpoint, can the West learn any communal benefits from Chinese techniques? The Western reliance on contract law and its enforcement (lawyers remain in demand but not necessarily in popularity) must adapt, toward a greater reliance on relational enforcement, by increasing trust and taking personal responsibility for actions. As any religious fanatic or convert will attest, faiths and beliefs are strong and directive. They dictate rational behavior within their own paradigm.

It is on the satisfaction of relational obligations, controlled by mutuality and the giving or exchange of personal respect (known as face), that the Chinese social paradigm is based. Their way of doing things deals nicely with contractual complexities. Now they can add Western legal niceties. Indeed, they can even use the legal wording to thwart foreign companies that do not have the right contacts. After all, protracted litigation in the West is not unusual. Twenty years on from the worst oil spill in Alaskan history, in March 1989, the Exxon Valdez, the local residents are still fighting in the US courts for compensation.

The Western demand for increased legal enforcement over contracts and agreements with China is really a demand for a Western paradigm. Yet the Western paradigm has failed – complex contractual governance is not resolved in court. Courts are for the simple man in the street, for the parking fine or fraud or murder; but to resolve complexity? Seldom.

The idea of the Chinese changing their methods is now seen to be wishful thinking. Chinese overseas will imitate Western ways, but not before testing and adapting them into a preferred hybrid version – imitative yet innovative. The corollary also holds that the

Anglo-Saxon should be more aware of high context behavior, relationship approaches and fluidity in task demands. Certainly, any alignment with the Middle East and Africa is a minor adjustment for the Chinese but a major adjustment for the West.

Hindsight also permits us to acknowledge that Western and Chinese societies have evolved at markedly different rates. Much of this has to do with technology and the very belated arrival of an industrial revolution in China. After the fiasco of 1793, when Lord Macartney was sent packing by Emperor Qing, who felt that China needed no baubles or trinkets from the British, a further century of mutual incomprehension passed, while various intrepid missionaries, traders and diplomats dimly perceived the extraordinary nature of this vast country, apparently sunk in stasis and immiseration. Traveling scholars and scientists from the West discovered to their immense surprise that China had invented and developed several ingenious and labor-saving devices long before similar devices had appeared in Europe. This prompted the inevitable question as to why the country had remained so underdeveloped.

Needham's Puzzle

A useful trigger to this debate on the whys and wherefores of China's apparent backwardness or arrested development is 'Needham's Puzzle'. Joseph Needham was a Cambridge University biochemist who became a devotee of China through his research. He worried this enigma into several volumes of exhaustive enquiry. Plainly stated, his grand question, his Puzzle, was this: given that China had the biggest economy in the world in the eighteenth century and an evident capacity for technological invention and bureaucratic control, why had the country not become a major power? Or, put another way, why did science and capitalism evolve in the West and not in China?

Interestingly enough, the classic and traditional Chinese answer to this Western question is disarmingly unexpected. It is twofold:

- Science had never been on the syllabus of the eight-legged examination for recruitment to the ranks of the civil administration. The scholar–official class thus remained ignorant or simply unaware of its potential; and

- The Chinese revere nature and viewed science as tampering with nature, and therefore harmful.

What is significant about these traditional answers is that they probably would not have occurred to Western thinkers or scientists, since they represent that peculiar cast of Chinese mind that sustained an effective and stable civil administration for over 2,000 years. The West routinely but simplistically ascribes China's apparent stasis to several perfectly plausible root causes, such as:

- Confucianism – and the static ordering of society and relationships.

- Demographics – the sheer number and density of people living off such limited natural resources.

- Education system – based on rote learning of classical texts rather than the nurturing of an enquiring mind.

- Natural disasters – earthquakes, famines, flooding, typhoons and epidemics.

- Male supremacy – the principle of favoring male over female.

- Subject status of all Chinese – with very tight limits on individual autonomy.

- Social mobility – severely restricted to those successful in the civil examination for entry into the scholar–official class.

- Face/public esteem – held in higher regard as a mark of social standing/status than mere money and wealth acquired through commerce.

However, the most probable reason is the precise inverse of this last factor:

- Low esteem for, and hostility to, the merchant class.

This meant that China did not harness until the late nineteenth century the power of free international trade and investment, since it lacked and is still largely deficient in the institutional infrastructure for economic exchange, ownership and accountability that is taken for granted in a pluralist society. They have not, as the West might judge it, a proper framework for contract law.

A major inference from this missed opportunity is that Western capitalism did not arise as an early driving force in Chinese society, simply because money was taken to be a part of the spoils and entitlement of office. Capital was acquired passively rather than actively through corruption and by 'clipping the ticket', and rarely by personal endeavor and industry. At the same time, it may also be deduced that institutional rigidities have impeded, and continue to impede, the development of a market economy. It is not communism that holds China back, but the remnants of imperial bureaucracy fixed in the mind of the individual and in the centralized governing controls of the Party hierarchy.

An imperial societal solution

The Chinese way of doing things, however, is traditionally derived from practice. In discussing the philosophical history of the Chinese, the most important aspect of the Chinese mind is that it tends towards practice rather than theory. Misunderstandings will arise when a Westerner explains a move from theory to practice. The best way to convince the Chinese of a theory's applicability is to set an example, then provide theory to explain the example, then another deduced example to confirm the pattern. Otherwise a description of a theoretical set of general events makes it difficult for any Chinese to establish the particular related event. It is foolish to rely on Western logic systems to do the arguing.

The Chinese operate in an inductive fashion, having no history of thinking comparable to Aristotelian logic or Wittgenstein's truth tables. The problem with induction, which has worried modern Western philosophers from David Hume to Karl Popper, is not seen by the Chinese as a problem. They accept that particular events are likely to form a pattern for future events. This should be borne in mind when discussing propositions. As noted already, Western practice is deductive, Chinese practice is inductive.

In fact, Chinese thought processes are much more in tune with the observations of David Hume, the great eighteenth-century Scottish moral philosopher, whose writing even now seems to distil the more commonsensical notions of the Enlightenment, particularly his description of 'impressions' as the ultimate basis for reasoned action and behavior. Indeed, Hume is the forerunner of Thomas Kuhn's much acclaimed paradigm theory, a theory where paradigms are firmly based on communal faiths and beliefs. Hume saw these 'impressions' as necessary to stop an infinite regress in arguments, and Kuhn saw scientists' faiths and beliefs as being necessary to develop and advance their arguments.

Chinese society has its own faiths and impressions to develop and advance its arguments, believing in the cultural practice of mutual obligation (*renqing*) – less a scratching of bilateral backs and more a relational need to achieve a dependency on one another. A dependency to prevent untoward opportunism from arising is deemed not only useful but necessary. In a domestic environment, where economic exchange is neither state-assisted nor yet contractually enforced in its outcome, the creation of natural reciprocity is the practical result of dealings among individuals and between networks.

A problem then lies with the extent to which such interdependency can be manipulated. When an obligation, a future option, is created through a relatively inexpensive gesture, then the reciprocal future obligation may still be called in an expensive manner. The benefits of preventing such behavior by meeting mutual needs and obligations are ensured by the simple strategy of paying one's debts immediately they are due. Reciprocal arrangements are not normally specified from the outset. The size of the debt and the future timing of its collection could be punitive. It cannot be deduced.

In China, obligations result from the acceptance of an initial benefit or gesture. While refusal of any offering will offend, the speedy reciprocation with your own gift of similar or equivalent value is essential. Honor is satisfied. Continue to work on the basis of past events creating the relational pattern for future events – Western ways are too testing.

The upwardly social middle classes

Problem-solving by the individual depends on three primary factors: emotion, social context and uncertainty. Emotion is best controlled in a group situation – by the stiff upper lip of the English army regiment, the shrug of the French shoulders, for example.

Conflict within the group, in the social context, creates a dilemma, the solution to which can be dangerous to others. The Bahasa Malay term 'to run amok' describes the disastrous effects of individual emotion overrunning the confines of the social *kampong*, the native village.

Will the Chinese run amok in the new world order? The social world of their childhood traditionally inculcates a certain collective responsibility, an instinctual interdependency. The more individualist West encourages a person toward a freedom of choice, mobility and action constrained only by relative loyalty, affection or dislike, and the law. But China has a pressing problem of individuals in a collectivist society. The single child policy from the 1980s is now a reality for single adults. Where is the socialization of the family in modern China? Chinese youth are less constrained and more spoilt than any previous generation. Will they see Western ways as the answer to a lack of brothers and sisters, to a void in traditional behavioral controls? Will they understand that Western individualism is both societal and familial – or will they see it as a panacea to their loss of Chinese tradition?

It is the lack of a larger family with brothers and sisters which could create a breakdown in traditional societal ways. Richer families are paying fines to have more children, and poorer rural families need hands on the farm, but the middle classes – those who are the mainstay of the Party hopefuls – are struggling with the principles of limited family sizes. Simple analysis will also show that a population that is not regenerating itself will not have sufficient future income to cover the costs of an aging population. This is happening in Japan and in the West but out of choice by the young. In China, there is not the luxury of choice. Our prediction is that the one-child policy will be relaxed in the usual step-by-step process. Pay the fine, turn a blind eye, avoid enforcement and then let it happen – claiming it was by decree all along.

Such legal sleight of hand is common in China. Lawyers attending to business with the Chinese are used to pointing out the weaknesses, but not the strengths, in legal enforcement. They do not expect any discussion to result in a beautifully drafted legal document. An agreement to agree is a useful device when China calls, as it serves to formulate a relationship. It is also the basis for further negotiation. A contract limits the bounds of further negotiation but does not end future options. Why spend a lot of cash on legally sound, but unenforceable, contracts when investment is better spent on the relationship – developing, maintaining and repairing it. Lawyers are best kept behind the scenes until really needed, their advice may then be adapted to the situation.

In an overseas environment, the Chinese can therefore become frustrated by the continuous quibbling of the legal profession. In such instances the legal experts should be introduced *at the end* of the negotiations. A competent diplomat or manager creating agreements or writing deals for his organization should understand basic legal principles. The lawyers may then tidy up any loose ends. Remember that the Chinese (as should all negotiators) look closely at the penalties in the contractual terms. As Shylock found out in Shakespeare's *The Merchant of Venice*, agreed damages may not be enforceable.

Confucian society

A return to Confucianism is a middle-class desire for traditional stability. Confucius lived in the state of Lu (present-day Shandong Province) from 551 to 479 BC, and was no prophet but rather a disappointed counsellor to local rulers. He despaired of constant warfare and civil strife, and retired at fifty to devise a means of restoring harmony to Chinese society. His teachings evolved from dialogues with disciples, and his wisest sayings are set down in his *Analects*.

Confucius can come across as an enigmatic snob, going on as he does about 'the superior man' but at his best he is superbly shrewd and wise. He is particularly disapproving of misbehavior in public and it is noted in his Analects that: 'respectfulness, without civilized behavior, becomes laborious bustle; carefulness, timidity; boldness, insubordination; straightforwardness, rudeness'. Hints of incivility in the West, when interpreted by the Chinese, will thus take on hues of cheek, cowardice, mutiny and bad manners.

Confucianism, however, is not a religion; rather it is a set of moral precepts, an ethical code designed to regulate the affairs of a state. It was not until the Han Dynasty (c. 200 BC to AD 200) that his teachings were adopted in practice and temples built in his honor.

His main teaching was that human relationships are naturally hierarchical – everyone must meet their obligations in these pre-determined or voluntary relationships, the *wu lun*: ruler/subject; father/son; husband/wife; elder brother/younger brother; friend/friend. Only the last is not immediately hierarchical.

Most interestingly, there is no provision in his teaching for dealing with strangers. The importance of these relationships is such that they define the position of the individual, the 'self', within Chinese society. The Chinese manager is therefore identified through his/her relationships – defining the allocentric, collectivist self. The foreigner must create a relationship to be identifiable. His or her corporation or organization is a good starting point – the juridical person will then slowly become the trusted individual.

Confucianism has provided a backbone of family values, respect for elders, civility, personal integrity and personal trustworthiness. The Chinese tendency to deal with familiar foreigners as 'old friends' rather than through contracts is a clear enough consequence of this. Indeed, Kevin Rudd, the prime minister of Australia, with his knowledge of Mandarin, is aware of the importance of being an old friend (*lao pengyou*), and his attitude to China aids Australian diplomacy. Unfortunately, Confucianism is also responsible for the Chinese inclination towards authoritarianism, denying subjects or subordinates any participation in decision-making (such as voting). The clash between Chinalco and RTZ is evidence of this, with retribution often sought by those at the top.

Loss of control

Another societal conclusion, within China, relates to a potential loss of control by the government. It takes very little for promises to remain unfulfilled. There are some making money, but many more in the rural areas are not. People's expectations are higher than the planned economy can provide. Shanghai old town, for example, is rapidly disappearing under construction sites. Hard hats are so common that the younger engineers wear them, like baseball caps, back-to-front.

Across the river from the historical Bund, the financial district in Pudong is more Tokyo than Tianjin, less Mao and more Marunouchi (the main commercial district of Tokyo). The shopping mall, with its super brands, is quite magnificent. The office ladies and Shanghai salarymen go there and eat in sushi bars and ramen restaurants. But when Beijing decides it's time for anti-Japanese rhetoric, those bars and restaurants stay empty – at least for an acceptable number of days. Once the political point is made, the queues re-form.

Such mass movement at the crook of a finger creates a conundrum. What if the economic miracle fails to cascade down to the majority of the Chinese people? What if political powers call for another sacrifice and are turned down? In overhead signs at Shanghai airport, the authorities make it clear that penal law is being enforced to allow 'the harmonious development of economic prosperity'.

Beijing airport is more legalistic and often warns the local populace (in Chinese) and foreigners (in English) of the sections and sub-paragraphs of statutes governing the policing of borders. Ignorance of the law is certainly no defense, but a belief that such red neon notices are required smacks of fear, not fortitude. Does the foreigner, or national citizen, need to be reminded constantly that the law is there to be obeyed?

And that fear will, ultimately, prevent democracy gaining a firm foothold in society. Trust, outside *guanxi*, is terrifyingly low. When asked to vote between Party members, any normal citizen says no – they do not wish to find themselves in a situation over which they have no control. Until a satisfactory opposition can be formed, so that a vote is between policies, not people, democracy will come a long way behind *guanxi*. In fact, most people with a vote are told what to do. Chinese votes are cast in the harmonious development of democracy. Such traditional leanings slow any form of democratic process in China. Is democracy then an impossible dream? Probably not, but certainly it will be culturally difficult to implement.

As a final comment on Confucian society, let us look at the alternatives. Chinese culture is not derived solely from Confucius. The feminine yin and masculine yang; Buddhism; Daoism, the fatalist view; *feng shui* – the superstitious matching of the flows, literally relating to 'wind' and 'water'; all serve to set out the singular and quite distinctive characteristics of Chinese cultural controls. It is the mixing and matching of disparate ideas for society that mark out traditional Chinese attitudes to life. External challenges such as Roman Catholicism are viewed with suspicion as being non-traditional and are not accommodated.

In the absence of a strong legal system but in the presence of strong tradition, the Chinese penalty is ostracism – as damaging as excommunication by the Pope. What might therefore constitute libel or slander and grounds for a Western law suit is, in China, as nothing compared with the visible and audible damage inflicted to the reputation and *amour propre* of the person affected, when witnessed at first hand by others. What in the West might be lived down with a self-deprecating laugh becomes in China a matter for memorably poignant recrimination. Dueling, on a point of honor, would be the closest Western analogy. Any failure to acknowledge the status of senior official or to consult with a particular authority in seeking approvals will never be forgotten – such is the power of the established society of doing and being.

Overseas, however, the established order is different. One of our respondents, working in the UK, notes that Western self-deprecation allows her considerable leeway in the learning process: 'Well, when I talk to the British I don't really care about looking silly [laughing] but … honestly … when in China I am concerned very much about my performance.' Western liberty creates a faster search for solutions; face is less of a problem within a protective legal structure. Ostracism is a personal Chinese punishment, not so easily communicated in the West, where the shoulder shrug indicates the 'whatever' of youth.

Language and knowledge in society

There are few distinct tenses in the usage of Chinese verbs. The tense is indicated more by qualifying adverbs than by suffixes. Hence the general sense conveyed is that of living in a kind of historic present. We recognize that the Chinese revere the past and that they go forward looking backward. This burden of harmony through time is borne by the use of proverbs and parables in speech, and pictographs in their written language.

Two issues are important to remember:

- The question of time becomes very subjective. The past, present and future are not immediately part of the grammatical construction. Indeed, it is worth considering that time overlaps in Chinese thinking. Western concepts of time are related primarily to equations involving simultaneity. The four dimensions of space–time are needed to specify an event. The Chinese search for harmony (rather than truth) requires language to be less specific (even tending to obfuscation), and space and time are flexible constructs. Western women are not averse to compressing time – such as counting each year after their twenty-first birthday as composed of twenty-four months. In such a case, a Western male emphasizing the number of lunar orbits to an earthly one quickly learns the opposite of harmony.

- Anecdotes are the means of revealing and making meaning clear between Chinese and Western managers when abstract concepts are discussed. Just as Christian parables have served as examples of conceptual thought, so the Chinese manager is able to understand meaning much more easily through practical vignettes (a visual story board) rather than hermeneutic analysis of sentences and descriptions.

Knowledge is gained qualitatively in China, primarily through the eyes and ears, within societal gatherings. How to use that knowledge is derived from the sixth sense – intuition. A small, easily solved problem is often used to begin discussion of the real issues at hand. Indirect communication maintains harmony and only by using the simple problem to generate trust will the larger problem and its attendant difficulties be discussed and resolved.

Guanxi – the Chinese problem solver

There is much smoke and there are many mirrors in the discussion of *guanxi*. Tapping the term into an internet search engine provides thousands of references. Many undervalue *guanxi* and others deem it to be overrated. One thing is for certain, it is more misunderstood than any other Asian custom or practice.

There are three basic factors to *guanxi* that are essential to remember in order to understand how Chinese society works, relates and controls:

- *Guanxi* is a dynamic system for the exchange of material resources and of information (knowledge). It eases transactions but helps to control opportunistic behavior. It improves resource allocation and aids resource development. It helps in deciding when it is worth beginning the initial investment into someone else's network.

- Face (*mianzi*) is transferred through a *guanxi* transaction, and reciprocity is created through mutual obligation (*renqing*). Harmony is the purpose. If face is cheap compared to the obligation, then a debt may not be repaid, and ostracism is minor. Harmony has a value adjustment in terms of pricing the transfer of *mianzi* against the cost of *renqing*.

- *Guanxi* networks protect the Chinese individual from penal law (and have done so for many centuries). The networks are therefore retained as relational protection against inadequate law enforcement. They are also retained within government as a political defense system. Seeking aid for a problem by entering another network for assistance is not unusual. The Westerner asks accountants, lawyers and friends for help. The relational problem, however, is that the cost of entry to a Chinese network is not immediately covered by a credit card or cash. A future option is created and manipulation through that option is common.

There are three things necessary to understand in China – *guanxi, guanxi* and *guanxi*. Each of the three is different but explicable. Consider *guanxi* as a dynamic system for controlling Chinese society. Understand it and interpret it accordingly. It is not magic. It has a Western mirror image in terms of good or gentlemanly behavior.

But it can be a tricky matter. The local politicians can see their future options running out when their positions become open for appointment. Gain what you can while you can. Peasants know who owns which paddy field from historic *guanxi*. There is a clash when the protection from past penal law is insufficient to protect the family from future appropriation of traditional land holdings. The political rural network has no obligation to the peasant network at a local level. Central authority is ensconced elsewhere.

The student and business mandate

It is anticipated that there will be 6–7 million students graduating each year up to 2015 in China. Many will struggle to find jobs that match their education. One immediate area of attraction and potential cross-over fusion with the West is the Master of Business Administration (MBA) program, which might be more aptly called a Makeover in Business Arts or conversion course in capitalist stratagems for Chinese youth. A main centre of learning in China is the CEIBS (the China–Europe International Business School in Shanghai) where novices are exposed to the esoteric arts of accounting and marketing, and the strange new science of management. However, the real value of such a novelty for the Chinese is the extended period of study they may enjoy at business schools in Europe and the USA.

The chief deficit to be made up by them is in marketing, largely because of the relative lack of branding in their products (a legacy of subcontracted manufacture for Western brands) and in the poor variety of choice in their domestic market. Unlike Western Europe or the USA, China is keen to transfer management thinking by encouraging overseas learning by students. Chinese universities are now producing too many graduates, who are complaining of the lack of opportunity. The card up the sleeve remains the overseas student. Jobs are scarce and many students are taking Master's courses in English-speaking universities (and in France and Germany). A satisfactory English assessment test (or foreign language pass) gains them entry to an overseas university and parents of a single-child family find the cash for their only offspring. The future Chinese Master will be in corporate management and financial engineering rather than in kung fu. The most productive step that Western companies can now take is to offer work experience and jobs to young Chinese graduates. Employing them overseas first means that the Chinese connections, contacts and colleagues would subsequently develop in China, lowering the entry barriers.

The modern overseas Chinese businessman is fluent in the language of his or her host country and its commerce, is well trained, educated and highly aware of the global marketplace, its benefits and its shortcomings. Whether representing a state-owned organization or an entrepreneurial enterprise, Chinese managers have a newly acquired sense of spirit tempered only by their seniors' traditional reluctance to make waves beyond a Chinese breakwater. Technological and internet advances are enabling expatriates to retain their Chinese hierarchy while extending their relationships overseas.

For now, the Chinese are spoilt for choice in terms of international partnerships on their domestic turf. The rate of increase in foreign direct investment may be easing, but not its magnitude. The Chinese continue to gain Western knowledge both at home and overseas. That knowledge is being put to good use, to gain resource control and to advance a global China.

Building society's bridges

However, rather than merely becoming more Western, the Chinese will adapt new tools and practices to maintain their loci of control over operations. The present trends are indicative of several bridges across the divide between West and East: broader ownership through flotations and acquisitions; lower hierarchical structures with increasingly dispersed managerial decision-making; promotion based on abilities within a group structure; task orientation but under broad guidelines; diversification for knowledge transfer but with a focus on opportunities; contracting out formal legal and accountancy systems while retaining internal network cash controls; and a mix of internal and external financing.

The hybrid Chinese organization is like modern Chinese society: more adaptive, more aggressive, more focused and more capable of finding solutions to new problems than in the past. Consider Taiwan as a controlled Chinese experiment in financial and democratic freedom, a small sample of a larger population and problem, financially successful but democratically fraught, with the political experiment now subject to considerable introspection.

The twentieth century, it must be remembered, opened, closed and reopened China's gates. It brought the dissolution of the imperial edict and its civil service under Sun Yat-sen, the Greater Co-Prosperity Sphere of the Japanese occupation brought more external oppression, the civil war laid bare both nationalist and communist ideologies, and the Age of Reform is now swiftly eroding tradition. We cannot blame the Chinese for craving more contentedness without further drastic changes.

We are seeing the societal values of the Chinese becoming considerably more adaptable. This adjustment is networked and institutional in its importance. Increased network flexibility and greater adaptability are a consequence of globalization and the attendant different ways of doing things. The implications are, thereafter, for individuals attuned to a non-hierarchical structure to assert themselves forcefully at a time of economic expansion. And we emphasize forcefully.

As far as forceful Chinese values are concerned, personal values such as those composing power distance (the kowtow, the tugging of the forelock) are no longer in tremble mode and are beginning to challenge the *status quo*. Important values are changing, with a significant increase in the importance of adaptability. An increase in the overall level of personal desires, coupled with a decrease in moderation and with lesser importance attached to prudent behavior, all paint, at first sight, a rather alarming picture of Chinese aggression.

Even at second sight, the thought of imprudent, immoderate, avaricious but adaptable Chinese managers creating a competitive advantage over Western counterparts should rattle what is left of Wall Street and the City. This is not a land of cheap labor but rather a country of commercially astute businessmen. On reflection, of course, we recognize the recent changes as being merely imitative. But it is a powerful imitation that is occurring.

Homecoming

Official estimates show that some two-thirds of Chinese who have studied abroad since the 1980s have elected not to return to work in China. Jobs at graduate level were not easy to find. At the time of writing, the Chinese diaspora worldwide has reached some 35 million in 150 countries. This tide, with new growth in China, is turning but demand will continue for Westerners and for Asians holding expatriate expertise. Foreigners make up the skills deficit in areas of expertise which have simply not been developed to the more exacting requirements of international trade, manufacturing and investment.

There will thus be a need to recruit an increasing number of qualified foreigners over the short-to-medium term, to lift the level of core competencies across the board – initially in areas such as banking, insurance, investment management, broking, accounting, actuarial practice, management consulting, manufacturing and engineering quality control, sales, product branding and marketing, and business planning. As the main urban conurbations become more crowded and polluted, there will be an equally pressing demand for experts in environmental protection, town planning and surveying, transport and communications, disease control and treatment, and the regulatory control of markets.

These skill gaps, according to the Asian counsel of an international mining company, have resulted chiefly from the Chinese education system of rote learning, which discourages the questioning of teachers and thus the development of enquiring minds. It is the capacity to think critically that is needed most keenly, the ability to form and present an independent view, to make a case for a certain course of action, strategy or tactic. This is particularly important in the acceptance of, for example, a successful technology transfer. A cadre of middle management needs to be created and developed in Chinese companies and joint ventures to ensure the effective communication and implementation of production, quality control, distribution and marketing plans and processes.

The teething troubles of such companies as Volkswagen in China, with quality control issues, and in the acrimonious joint venture between Danone and Wahaha, can be traced to poor levels of middle management. Risk management is another key area, where foreign banks used to play a role but now look less than expert. Domestic Chinese have hitherto been accustomed to receiving and spending working capital and loans from state banks without proper accountability. The Western opacity of the 'slice, dice and splice' debt packages hold no fear for the Chinese, even though these paperless transactions are now quite disreputable.

The graduates are heading overseas on Master's programs but are also complaining of a lack of practical education. The Chinese demand for overseas experience of a non-theoretical nature will not result from Western educational systems but from Western organizations and institutions. The overseas Chinese postgraduate may be welcomed home but prefers to remain overseas. Practical overseas experience will increase the opportunities for Chinese networks to expand on a global basis.

Their civil engineers are using Africa as a training ground for the infrastructure and civil engineering projects required in China. Returning after a year or so, they can set about rebuilding China, having served their overseas apprenticeships. Financial and marketing abilities are being honed in New York and London. Democracy, we have already argued, is an observable, possibly failed, experiment in Taiwan. China knows that technology transfer is nothing to inward skills transfer. And modern skills are now led by overseas Chinese. Over a million Taiwanese are estimated to be working in (or should it be on?) China. Inward skills are in manufacturing, electronics and contractual techniques with foreign buyers.

Now take away the figures and the rhetoric and remember that the Chinese government, since the Reform, has emphasized the concepts of *fa zhi* (rule by law) and *ren zhi* (rule by people) within China. These concepts will, of course, be slow to process through the bureaucratic machinery, and are still being engineered and fine-tuned. The interim stage means that contacts continue as the time-honored way of getting things done. Even when a lawyer is paid with a handsome fee, the Chinese would still feel that they have a future obligation to a successful advocate. It is in the nature of the network.

Chinese societal behavior

Just as *guanxi* has three major facets, so Chinese behavioral choices are governed by *qing*, *li* and *fa*. Human feelings, *renqing*, are explained earlier in the book and imply relational obligation. The *wu li* are five (*wu*) ordered hierarchical relationships (*li*). The rules or laws or principles are denoted by *fa*. In China these three choices of behavior are in a strict order. That suggests that whatever happens in China, *qing* is the first option that one should take. The ordering of those feelings is dictated by *li*. Thus the Chinese tradition means that government and national (as opposed to communally networked) rules or *fa* fall last in line. The conscientious objector would follow *qing* well before enforced *fa*.

Feelings, no matter the hardship, are traditionally considered first and are designed to maintain happiness and harmony in the networked group. The order of things may change, however, during periods of chaos, and that represents an opportunity in Chinese society – a breakdown allowing freedom. And enforced regulations, if at all complex, will lead to some ambiguity and afford protection if one is connected. It is not possible therefore to make a predictable conclusion from a moral and social value system that depends on hardship for happiness, on chaos for opportunity, and on complexity for protection. The more that is known about the Chinese, the less is understood. But be assured that hardship, chaos and complexity fit better with *qing*, than with *fa*.

However, the Chinese are of a less moderate but more adaptable disposition in an international context. The need to apply integrated, not piecemeal, Western ideas must be met when trying to deal with Chinese practices, both domestic and global. Flexibility through holistic, non-confrontational strategies is the only solution. Threatening the Chinese with sanctions or tariffs simply signals that any mutual relationship is off limits. It is Western consumerism that made the Chinese powerful; it is the West that opened the Asian door. Reciprocity is the key to a two-way flow.

Concentrate on the contexts and specifications governing the rules of Chinese social systems. Try to adapt or change the context, not the rules, because the rules for the Chinese always follow the context. The perceived authority of the Western context is insufficient to command anything beyond that demanded by manners, mutual respect and reciprocity of action. Poor Western behavior quickly transforms the relationship into mutual distrust and subsequent retaliatory action. The transformation caused by ignorant Western interaction is seen in the behavioral changes in Chinese society. The short-term consideration rather than the long-term obligation enables a less moderate style of doing things to grow in practice.

The need for high trust levels when forming a long-term relationship remains, but the frequency of short-term relationships is increasing. Global trust is not a common commodity outside a known network. Unlike the individualistic West, the Chinese have very low levels of trust beyond their peripheries. A negotiated compromise, an arbitrated level of governance, is needed. The Chinese will not take the lead; they prefer to follow the rules as practiced.

So what do we see in Chinese society as it globalizes? First, the Chinese use reciprocity and risk in their thinking, and consider them to be linked to problem-solving. You cannot have one without the other when maintaining a relationship. Second, and perhaps more importantly, the Chinese see holistic solutions to a problem as a group and social necessity. All must be catered for – not just one individual. The Chinese seek an integrated, group-dominated solution. Third, and as a further explanation, decisions regarding the family, and especially family loyalty, are becoming directed towards money. Modern Chinese may be turning, dare we say it, American, in their search for a yellow (golden) brick road.

The Chinese have been letting market forces become significantly more important than traditional collective controls. Increases in external, foreign forces are associated with a decrease in internal group pressures. Conformity was beginning to go. Chinese society was slowly changing, but the benefits of gaining Western ideas, whether democracy or the law, are now put on hold because of the present strength of domestic control by senior politicians in China. The modern Chinese are dependent on the degrees of freedom delegated from the top, and these remain restrictive.

The West, with its failures well recognized – financially, politically, militarily, socially – has lost the credibility and moral authority to transform Chinese society. The Chinese will therefore maintain their basic societal ways of doing things but will start a partial but aggressive adjustment to world affairs. Better to take control of the sought-after international resource, either by acquisition or merger or might before the West damages it. Compromise is feasible, but ambiguity in Chinese society is likely to increase in the short term, making Western interpretation confusing. Chinese adjustment will be truly challenging, but it will be internally driven. The opportunity to guide China from the outside is probably lost: it is China that will decide its own destiny.

Points to ponder

Points

Part I provides our personal assessment of the divergence in Western and Eastern mentalities, and a means of understanding the Chinese by considering the basic network rules of their behavioral system. We emphasize how their thinking and problem-solving depend on Chinese views on uncertainty – and their finely calculated approach in the evaluation of future risk via understanding and using relationships, their *guanxi*.

The West must acknowledge that the global rules have changed. Chinese state-owned enterprises were allowed under strict government investment criteria to invest overseas. Since 2003, private companies have also been able to do so. The pace of investment overseas is thus changing rapidly because of the political and institutional alterations within China. It is not, therefore, merely the suitability or acceptability of an overseas market that has occurred (through World Trade Organization entry, for example), but also the time change in the granting of permission from the Chinese authorities. The acceleration of Chinese overseas investment is both timely and dominant in two areas – Africa and Asia-Pacific.

China is thus taking the opportunity to increase its resource control in Africa and to extend protective border controls in Asia-Pacific. The nature of global exchange makes such specific overseas investment by China not only desirable but also essential to secure the needs of Chinese society. At the present time, the forgotten continent of Africa remains on the periphery of Western vision. The Chinese reciprocal relationship, high context communication and their 'gift-giving' predilections make for an automatic match with many African anti-Western governments.

Short-term Chinese opportunism in Africa means immediate assistance to African governments needing commercial essentials – factory output and bills of exchange. Long-term control over commodities essential to Chinese growth is the ultimate aim. In Sudan it is oil; infrastructure in Kenya; minerals, hotels, transport, equipment and more in Zimbabwe, Algeria, Angola, and into a host of nations desperate for recognition and reward. In South America, it is oil, timber and fish; the Amazon rainforest, perforce, is now being logged and marked 'Made for China'.

Nothing will be sacred – take the Westernized World Food Program as a further potential gift-giving target. The US control over aid to the starving ensures good prices for American wheat and American ships. If China were to enter the grain markets in a really big way – to feed its people better – the pricing economics of basic resources then move rapidly through the supply chain. Agricultural prices are taking off and Africa is likely to starve without Chinese help.

The nature of Chinese reciprocity allows an affinity with the African (helped by no history of Chinese colonialism) to exchange maize for minerals and rice for mining rights. Cash is exchanged for a present obligation – to be called on later. The extent of Chinese penetration into the global marketplace is underestimated. Economic colonization by China is a product of Western intransigence. Mining resources, and their rise in Western stock and commodity markets, are mirrored in China, but for Chinese oil and financial stocks. The World Bank positively endorses the lessons of China's transformation policy for Africa. One of their African vice-presidents, Oby Ezekwesili, is reported to have said (*China Daily*, March 20, 2008) that Chinese assistance is of a nature that helps African citizens to take advantage of globalization. The incentives offered by China are fundamental, she pointed out, and that 'it does not matter from which part of the world they come from'.

The Chinese are, ultimately, bringing African (as well as South American and Middle Eastern) governments into a barter trading pattern, ensuring the long-term future of Chinese factories, fields and population. Present global problems are a result of Western consumerism, but future issues will be of Chinese economic demand. Chinese domestic demand will trigger Western inflation and increase, rather than decrease, friction in global trade. After all, what consumer hardware does the West make that the East actually wants?

China is therefore intent on binding relations with the two richest resource hubs on the planet – close to home is Siberia with its largely untapped trove of oil and minerals (with Mongolia, still a vassal state rich in copper and coal, straddling the borderlands) and further afield is the Middle East and 'Persian' Gulf, with its abundant oil stream. To the south, Australia and Indonesia are key sources of liquid natural gas. For the present, hydroelectric stations and coal will provide the bulk of home-grown power generation. Coal will continue as a major industrial fuel until around 2030, and will result in environmental damage.

Two features stand out from this summary of Chinese ways of doing things and their resultant global aspirations. First, the essential practicality and pragmatism of the Chinese approach versus the more abstract and theoretical construct of the West; and second, the 'bottom-up' thrust of applied Chinese values versus the 'top-down' drive of enforced Western law.What happens if we can join these two systems? The overseas Chinese expatriate returning to China will make different decisions from domestic colleagues. He or she will seek profitability by minimizing wasteful resource usage. Formal techniques of managing and doing will include investing based on calculated returns on capital, corruption will be frowned on but not eliminated, and the environment, education and the family's future will drive economic demands. Contentedness is not merely owning a color television.

So why will China not follow the same course as its capitalist neighbor, Japan? One answer is the lack of democracy – buying votes through over-stimulation of the economy is unnecessary. Another answer is the strong family value system in China, so that a *kowtow* to the government or its institutions is unlikely. China's overseas expansion will absorb much of the domestic heat. The government's engineers love infrastructure projects: have theodolite, will travel; have heaps of cash, will travel far. There are also demands on the Chinese to comply with international legal and accounting practices, especially given the recent increase in companies listed on overseas stock exchanges.

Conflict is possible where traditional relational control over economic exchange is superseded by legally enforceable contracts and financial reporting standards. But what is it that causes potential conflict? In two words: Western consumerism. Consumers create demand, and demand makes money for Western governments – why else have taxes on goods and services? China meets any demand, banking the Wal-Mart shopper. But the debt from the West, the Chinese dollar dues, must be paid. The debt due from the USA to China is now large enough to create problems for China.

Ponder

China is faced with a strategic dilemma. How does a society, firmly entrenched in the communal family adapt to a market economy? A trial and error market is in conflict with the tried and tested societal relationship, as shown in Figure I.1.

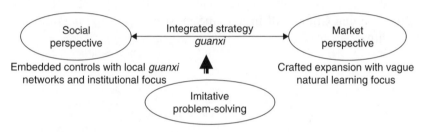

Figure I.1 Social equilibrium.

The Chinese future can be interpreted as balancing the tension between domestic societal needs and the global integration necessary for applying economic and military expansion. Change and adaptation will be achieved mainly through imitating the West. Yet the West has so far failed to apply its own expertise successfully. China will copy from its own past as well as from the West. Slowly but inexorably, China's traditions will alter to resolve the problem Chinese-style. Creating its own markets is not merely a case of domestic consumer demand. Chinese control in the commodity markets is an essential Chinese strategy to ensure the full flow of domestic productivity.

And to control the servicing of those commodities and resources, the Chinese will imitate the Western military. Where does the Western military strategy now concentrate? It is adapting away from the Cold War and on to counter-insurgency, not merely the big-ticket items of nuclear submarines, but a focus on guerrilla techniques and technological advances in the gathering of intelligence.

It is here that the ongoing process of trial and error will allow the justification of experiment and the adaptation of present values and beliefs. Globalization is not a Western standardization of hamburger, cola and fries. It is a unique stage in world progress (colonialism was not globalization) and it is one that will be categorized by heterogeneity, not homogeneity. The Chinese are well placed to copy Western anti-insurgency techniques in Afghanistan and to use that knowledge in Xinjiang and Tibet. In many respects, the West sets an example, but just as you should be careful what you wish for, you must also be careful what example you set. Time will tell whether Western examples are good or bad for global stability. The odds are that China will imitate the most useful to the benefit only of China.

PART II

Power, opportunities, equilibrium, military, science

Reason is nothing but a wonderful and unintelligible instinct in our souls, which carries us along a certain trait of ideas, and endows them with particular qualities, according to their particular situations and relations.

(David Hume, *A Treatise of Human Nature*, Book I, Sect. XVI)

Introduction

The Middle Kingdom's purview on the world and on the West, in particular, is inevitably colored by the deep historical hurt it feels. The West – in the shape of the European maritime powers and later the Americans – had no business to come marauding into China in the late eighteenth and early nineteenth centuries to force it into foreign trade. This is why the flashpoints of protest that erupted over Tibet and the Olympic torch relay in the summer of 2008 were like salt rubbed into the raw wound of Chinese hypersensitivity to any outside questioning of its territorial integrity. The Dalai Lama's meeting with President Nicolas Sarkozy of France was grounds enough for cancellation of the annual EU–China Summit, urgently awaited as an opportunity to address China's huge trade surplus and a fully co-ordinated approach to the global financial crisis. The hurt of historical humiliation runs so deep that a litany of dastardly acts is still consistently cited as a reminder of Western misdeeds.

China's view of the West

The trading relations that are now enjoyed have come about at a heavy cost to China by its own reckoning. It was not until the early 1800s that the Chinese emperor and his scholar–officials became sufficiently concerned about foreign countries to undertake any thorough investigation of their situations and cultures. Chinese ports opened for the first time to US merchant ships in 1784, just a few years after the American Revolution and ahead of the abortive trade mission of Britain's Lord Macartney in 1793. But it was not until the infamous Opium Wars in the 1830s – in which Britain found and forced on the Chinese a commodity acceptable to trade with them – that any real commercial and social engagement occurred.

There followed the ingloriously unequal Treaty of Nanking in 1842, under which the island of Hong Kong was ceded to the British as a trading base 'in perpetuity'; the Boxer Rebellion of 1900; the sacking of Beijing and the burning of the Summer Palace by British and French troops; and then, the final straw, the Peace Treaty of Versailles in 1919, under which large areas of Shandong, formerly held by the Germans, were made over to the Japanese. By this time, the tide of outraged feeling in China had reached a high-water mark, and revolutionary fervor had gripped the country, desperately anxious to avoid further humiliation and to get a hold on its own destiny. To the West, China was seen as a pushover, by the Europeans as woefully unprepared for any serious military engagement, and by the Americans as a booby nation – all of which was profoundly demeaning and wounding to China's self-esteem.

The spontaneous student uprising at the news of China's heavy loss of face with the Versailles Treaty in 1919 came to be known as the May 4th Movement. One of its leaders, Chen Duxiu, proclaimed that their mission was 'to import the foundation of Western society, that is, the new belief in equality and human rights … We must be thoroughly aware of the incompatibility between Confucianism and the new belief, the new society and the new State … Be cosmopolitan, not isolationist … He who builds his cart behind closed gates will find it not suited to the tracks outside the gates'. But the new president, Sun Yat-sen, demurred: he feared that a rupture with Chinese tradition would uproot the country's political system and make governing a unified state impossible in the wake of the imperial order. Instead, he proposed opening China up to Western investment and technology, to create a modern empire to rival the West's. 'We must', he said, 'take England as our model and must extend England's example of good government to the whole of China.'

Perhaps it is no wonder then that China is impatient with the European Union's (EU's) lack of unity, cohesion and unreadiness to speak with a single voice on many key issues, particularly the global banking crisis, and China is now in a position of sufficient strength politically to exploit this at little cost to itself. It continues to project an image of blatant self-interest and brutal lack of concern for basic human rights. This it justifies on the grounds that China differs significantly from the West in its historical, cultural and religious background, stage of economic development, political system and ideology. Specifically, it points to the special importance given to the Chinese ideal of interpersonal harmony, individual responsibility to a wider society, and the resulting need to balance individual and collective rights. In contrast, Western cultures are seen to attach greater importance to individuals' rights and personal preferences and freedoms, supposedly independent of, or in opposition to, their governance and obligations to society.

Although much light has been let in on China from the outside world via overseas travel, films, literature, foreign media and mobile communications, old attitudes still prevail among the Chinese populace; racist prejudice against darker-skinned peoples, xenophobia and a high level of crude stereotyping. Imperial attitudes persist: old concepts of the absolute superiority of China's civilization (and the unassailable primacy of the emperor) have made dealings with foreigners as equals almost impossible. Now that the Chinese Communist Party (CCP) is the surrogate emperor, it is not too difficult to understand how hard the imperial order and thinking dies. In their mind's eye, the walled world of their imagination is China's strongest redoubt, a firewall against further invasion of foreign influence and ideas, the physical symbol of continuity and endurance in the face of barbarism, crassness and vulgarity.

Telling it like it is

In the wake of the systems breakdown in world banking, China is crucially empowered to lead initiatives to ensure recovery and to restore confidence in financial institutions. Chief among these must be a common agreement for regulatory controls on mortgage lending, derivatives, short-selling and consumer debt – all areas where unfettered profligacy has led to catastrophic downfall. Gao Xiqing, president of China Investment Corporation, responsible for investing US$200 billion of the country's foreign exchange reserves (their Sovereign Wealth Fund), tells a rueful, cautionary tale:

> If you look at every one of these [derivative] products, they make sense. But in aggregate, they are bullshit. They are crap. They serve to cheat people ... [the State Council] wanted me to explain about capital markets and how they worked ... So I wondered, 'How do I explain derivatives?', and I used the model of mirrors. Someone says, 'I don't have to sell the [product] itself! I have a mirror, and I can sell the mirror image!' Okay. That's a stock certificate. And then someone else says, 'I have another mirror – I can sell a mirror image of that mirror.' Derivatives. That's fine too, for a while. Then you have 10,000 mirrors, and the image is almost perfect. People start to believe that these mirrors are almost the real thing. But at some point, the image is interrupted. And all the rest will go.

Premier Wen Jiabao announced that the Chinese budget deficit would be around US$150 billion in 2009. This is almost 20 per cent less than projected UK government borrowings in 2009/10. The cost of the collapse in Western banking can now be measured in terms of government spending on financial sector support as a percentage share of national gross domestic product (GDP) as follows: the UK's is by far the largest at almost 20 per cent, while that of the USA is a more modest 6.3 per cent and the German and French figures are 3.7 per cent and 1.5 per cent, respectively. It is hardly surprising that the Chinese found events and actions leading to this financial debacle little short of ridiculous.

The Central Bank governor, Zhou Xiaochuan, was unusually blunt in his assessment of US behavior: 'Over-consumption and a high reliance on credit is the cause of the US financial crisis … As the largest and most important economy in the world, the US should take the initiative to adjust its policies, raise its savings ratio appropriately and reduce its trade and fiscal deficits.' This also raised uneasy questions about when the RMB might become the world's reserve currency, as the dollar slides. There is a certain inevitability about this: as the US emerging markets guru, Mark Mobius, has predicted, 'The dollar will go the way of the Roman denarius.'

China will now insist on a more clearly defined role for the state in new market capitalism; and will demand a concerted effort among the 'CRIMB' countries (China, Russia, India, Middle East and Brazil) – so-called to reflect the new order of economic powers – to act as locomotives in the redirecting of the world economy.

Chinese young people's view of the West

There are many young Chinese studying overseas. They have a mixed view of each country they visit. One young female student enjoyed the big city lifestyle but reckoned that France was the best because 'They had a nudist beach – I loved it!' Many of them prefer the US accent because of their teachers of English in China. The inward interest in China from Western youth is increasing rapidly, and a month's course in teaching English as a foreign language lets many young Americans into China to learn Mandarin and earn money. Students are well to the forefront in visiting China and this bodes well for improved reciprocal understanding in the future.

Chinese youth in the UK have mixed views, depending on where they are studying. One tourist town with a redbrick (recent) university had an open-top sightseeing bus which tourists took to see the ancient monuments in the town. Local thugs and drunken youths decided this was an excellent bit of fun and threw litter at the student tourists and used foul language. This generational problem in the West exemplifies the loss of authority on the part of both parents and police. The West has moved from the traditions of its own past to the psychology of the victim. Tell a British youngster to stop throwing litter and the mobile phone-call to the police, claiming adult harassment, is to be expected. Lies and damned lies are difficult to dispute when youth is believed first and adults are treated with suspicion.

The Chinese find this lack of reverence for the older generation quite shocking. They believe that traditional ways still persist. The British Council was sufficiently interested in how the Chinese see the UK that they commissioned a report from a UK university. Professor Greg Philo interviewed Chinese students at Western universities and noted – as we have done – that they think that old beliefs and attitudes still persist. The British, for example, are seen as gentle, polite, kind and conservative. When questioned more closely, the students tend to admit that these impressions are based on literary classics such as *Pride and Prejudice* and the Sherlock Holmes stories rather than first-hand contact with British men and women.

Students are reluctant to criticize or to make unflattering comparisons between the West and China for fear of causing loss of face to parents or compatriots. The truth in China is often a closely guarded secret. But reality often brings a rude awakening, with prior expectations shattered by the drunk and disorderly behavior of young people. By contrast, students often found the manners of older people charming and wished that Chinese elders could be as gracious. A student living in one of the older university towns, the report noted, was convinced old values remained when a man stopped his car to let the student cross the road. Another was not amused, however, by the poorly educated drunks and vulgarity of young people in a provincial town.

There is certainly a fear of going out late at night. One student we interviewed said that it was harming her studies in the winter as she was frightened of leaving the library too late and having to walk home to her accommodation in the darkness. The report noted a disappointment in learning: 'I thought there would be something special in the culture, people would say interesting things. I thought it would be a *garden of thinking*.' How easily are attractive myths dispelled! Personal reminiscence calls to mind a conversation-stopper from Han Lih-wu, the KMT interior minister responsible for spiriting away the imperial treasures from Nanking to Taiwan, who had studied at the London School of Economics with Professor Harold Laski in the 1930s: 'And where are the Bertrand Russells of today?' he asked.

Overall, the students we interviewed and those interviewed in the report greatly admired the Western education system, the health and welfare services, and the arts and creative design. They were also pleasantly surprised at the multiculturalism of society, the extraordinary mix of peoples and ethnic groups in cities such as London and Paris. One student told us that once they knew how many other races were present on the course (Africans, North Americans, Europeans, Russians and Indians) they would recommend it to friends back in China. It is, if anything, the dispelling of xenophobic myths that the Chinese seem to benefit from. Through travel and understanding of other cultures and societies, the Chinese, and indeed all of us, benefit. Certainly the West will gain much by understanding China's more homogeneous and tight-knit ways and customs.

Finally, we summarize and quote examples from the British Council report, as it provides a useful juxtaposition of views from Chinese youth and sets off the examples we have taken from business and politics. They indicated to Professor Philo what they would like to take back with them to China, and mentioned the following:

- Breakfast – 'The way they eat breakfast. Gives a good feeling all day.'

- Good manners – and the ability to relax and enjoy leisure pursuits.

- Charitable events – as an element of public culture.

- Relief from personal anxiety – going out and meeting friends as opposed to staying in and fretting about a job, studies or parents.

- Health care – more availability in the UK, but as China becomes more market-driven, public services decrease and medical treatment becomes much more expensive and harder to get.

- Opportunities for women – seem better versus the 'beauty economy' in China, where employment is often determined by age and personal attractiveness.

- Civil and criminal law – contrasts greatly with the *guanxi* culture, defined by one student as a system of family, social, economic and political networks extending through every part of life in China.

- Education – encourages independent thinking and creativity. The Chinese learn by rote and need to memorize chunks from textbooks, but are not encouraged to ask questions or to think critically.

- Open media – greater press freedom: 'The media, including television programmes, newspapers and magazines are so open-minded to sex, political opinions and social issues.'

- Overcoming racial prejudice – the natural tendency of the Chinese to distrust foreigners is evident and tends to be based on irrational fear: 'I met some very smart, nice African people. Chinese people don't like black people. That changed my mind. I was so afraid of black people.'

Arts and crafts

The leading actors (politicians), in the drama of state development and the furtherance of national interest in the East and the West, differ widely in their social origins and in their educational backgrounds. The political class in Europe, for example, draws its members by and large from those who have studied the humanities – the classics, history, literature, law, philosophy and languages – with only a smattering of scientists. China's leaders are almost exclusively drawn from other cohorts and cadres, those who have worked as proven engineers, scientists, economists, managers and regional administrators – and won recognition as hard-hat practitioners of necessary transformation. The word in China is more closely allied with the deed. Like all scientists and engineers, they much prefer to 'walk the talk' in conversational exchanges geared to practical application of new policy initiatives rather than to engage in abstruse examination of policy options on paper, for prolonged debate.

These differences would appear to indicate a natural bent in China towards entrusting the business of law-making and the direction and supervision of the economy to practitioners in various technical disciplines, while in the West there is an inclination to entrust this business to philosophical thinkers and theorists. This is in part a reflection of the depth and quality of the public debate that is permitted or actively encouraged in the respective societies. In China, the debate is still seen as the preserve of an educated elite, whose paternalism does not include the advancement of a spirit of free enquiry into the nature and benefits of differing systems and forms of governance. For the moment, certainty prevails and doubt is put on hold as long as compulsory modules in Marxism–Leninism are still part of all university courses.

One way to loosen the shackles of straitened thinking might be to provide a level playing field of theoretical ideas as a world-wide basis of comparison. Readings of comparative literature are instructive and revelatory: extracts, say, from the Confucian *Analects* alongside the Opus Dei founder's tract by Jose Maria Escriva, *The Way*, and *The Aristos* (a digest of sayings and aphorisms from Western humanistic, philosophical teachings) by the British writer, John Fowles. This will guarantee a good mental work-out with its gentle balance of Confucian rationalism, faith-based design for living and first-hand contact with the humanism of Western antiquity – all fit perhaps to fill the void of a barren, post-Marxist epoch. It is also more likely to chime with a Chinese tradition of harmony and 'higher Socialism'. In addition, it might help to explain how and why Confucianism prevailed morally over competing Han forms of government such as Legalism, with its black and white formulation of controls and sanctions, which still find expression and outlet in present-day Singapore with its canings, Love Boats, summary executions and legalized prostitution.

Weighed in the balance

While Western yardsticks or measuring gauges of value are mainly quantitative, China's are largely qualitative. Achievement and advance in China is intuited via emulation and rated by the degree of successful imitation and improvement accomplished – in the arts as well as in manufacturing. The West's fixation on the performance of a company's quarterly earnings has led to a 'growth at all costs' capitalism, which has put a heavy premium on manipulative financial engineering skills at the expense of any real underlying value in a company's stocks or shares for the stakeholder. The breach of trust resulting from Western banks acting as portfolio managers with funds entrusted to them as deposits has proved to be almost irreparable.

The very notions of 'deposit' and 'savings' as account designations have been fundamentally altered and disfigured in the banks' headlong career to build bigger asset bases. European banks loaned an estimated US$3.5 trillion to the markets of emerging economies, compared with US$500 billion from the USA and US$200 billion from Japan. Three-quarters of loans to China and India have originated in Europe. In China, by contrast, the banking system is funded mainly by deposits, not capital markets. In addition, bank lending amounts to no more than 65 per cent of deposits. Ratios in the USA and Europe are much higher. More tellingly, household debt is only 13 per cent of GDP versus 100 per cent in the USA.

The gradual decline of US influence in the world can be measured in the steady fall of its share of global GDP since 2001. China's share is rising at such a rate that it will likely overtake the USA within a generation. China may also emerge from the financial crisis relatively unscathed, since it has none of the global toxic debts that are plaguing US and European banks. Its new model of capitalism can safely be exported to the developing world. Such is its financial strength that it could easily supplement the emergency credit lines currently available under International Monetary Fund quotas. However, its banks need central government control – just as they do in the West!

Executive summary

This part views the world from a Chinese standpoint, shows how China understands (and misunderstands) the West and provides some pointers for the course of future globalization and interdependency. It also indicates what the West can most profitably learn from the Chinese in terms of endeavor, risk-taking, discipline, sacrifice, resilience, patience, practicality and pragmatism. China is preparing itself as never before for a serious engagement with the very disparate and pluralistic societies of Europe and the USA. This cannot be achieved without both China and the West taking a truer measure of each other's terms. By doing so, other nations in Africa, Latin America and the Middle East will benefit from such positive guidance. This will allow much closer collaboration in our dealings and a much keener appreciation of each other's values and priorities.

1. *Power* unfolds the subtle nature of China's rising influence and global authority and the way in which it seeks to exert its position powerfully, but peaceably.

2. *Opportunities* indicate the key areas in which China uses its new-found wealth to extend sources of mineral and energy supply, funding its quest for knowledge, technology and cultural solidarity with the developing world in the Asia/Pacific region, Africa and Latin America.

3. *Equilibrium* depicts China's struggle to achieve a balance between humans and nature in the new environment created by its current energy supply predicament. It examines the challenge posed to the West by a mission to become a clean, green, global superpower.

4. *Military* delineates the largely defensive and protectionist role of China's armed forces as they deploy a strategy of tactical asymmetry in safeguarding its key commercial and security interests and its territorial integrity.

5. *Science* goes to the roots of China's ethical and moral codes and examines its current policy of scientific development. The mainsprings and stumbling blocks that have frustrated progress, and the steps being taken to remove such blocks, are highlighted.

Part II takes the reader forward into another perspective on China's development and global advancement. The perspective is one designed to allow an understanding of a society which has problems of internal trust. By seeking external assistance, China is creating opportunities for greater global interaction of a mutually beneficial nature, surprising some Western observers. This second part of the book examines the scope for expansion from a Chinese vantage point and the key elements for an effective Western response.

CHAPTER 6

Power

Our obsequiousness to our superiors more frequently arises from our admiration for the advantages of their situation, than from any private expectations of benefit from their goodwill.

(Adam Smith, *The Theory of Moral Sentiments (1759)*, p. 73)

Introduction

While the world would thrust the status of Great Power on China in the somewhat desperate hope that it will take up some of the world's locomotive slack, apparently over 80 per cent of the Chinese people don't believe or want to be involved in this. How can we be a *Da Guo* (Great Country), they say, when our per capita GDP is one-twentieth that of the UK. The political flashpoint events in Darfur and Lhasa and the Olympic torch relay protests in London, Paris and San Francisco in 2008 made the Chinese flinch and recoil in shock and outrage in the face of unprecedented close encounters with the weight and strength of international feeling. Tensions have since been eased in part by a mightily successful Olympic Games in Beijing and the first-hand contacts these generated.

Now, with the world's banking and financial crisis striking China much closer to home, the country is obliged to make immediate common cause with the West to stave off disaster in the world economy. Having to cut interest rates in alignment with other countries simply underlined this growing inter-dependency. At the same time, there is bewilderment at the fate of former teachers and mentors, the Western politicians and their economic advisors, who have stumbled so badly. There is thus also grave hesitation and uncertainty about the kind of lead that China should give in world affairs, now that it disposes of such political and financial power.

What is the nature of state power? Is it simply the capacity to exercise control and influence over the use of a country's common wealth and resources? Or has it sometimes rather more to do with influence, even dominion, over a citizen's mind? Thought-control is exerted by 'the authorities' to enforce a common will in pursuit of maintaining 'a collective personality'? Power, of course, is quite distinct from authority, which should be based on legitimacy and the right to exercise power according (in a democracy, at least) to the will of the majority of the people. It is essentially decision-making when it impacts upon the choices and direction of people's lives.

China's chosen path and policy direction is one of 'scientific development'. This seems to point towards a kind of systems engineering or application of mechanical processes to improve human organizational efficiency and productivity. Such an approach may involve aids to hasten these processes, such as artificial intelligence and the creation of silos of specialized technical knowledge. As a tenet of faith in a scientific revolution this belief harks back to President Kennedy's space programme to the moon (and back) or the 'white heat of technology' bombast of the Harold Wilson era in the UK in the 1970s.

Down below the parapet of rhetoric, what is in fact taking place to advance these grand designs? If power has any force to move minds – short of coercion, intimidation and the flexing of fear as instruments of control – it must be *relational* in nature. In a relatively more manageable state such as Singapore, people may more readily consider themselves stakeholders in a family enterprise – in spite of petty restrictions on their freedom of thought and expression. In China, however, the span of control is so tenuous that people may feel that government is so far removed from their daily lives as to be indifferent to their pressing concerns and welfare, thus rendering them ineligible to take part in the national conversation.

As in any contract or social compact, there must be offer and acceptance of key terms and ideas between the parties. Without this engagement or common vision, people will surely become disaffected and rebellious, because of the lack of any accountability. In short, there must be a sense of a balance of power held between rulers and ruled, a tipping of the scales into a tighter equilibrium, so that rulers can be held to account. With the demise of emperors and kings, the Mandate of Heaven is lost for ever, since absolute power is yielded up. Who is to share the spoils? From where is authority to be derived? The new People's Republic in China has brought immense emancipation for its people, and deep and lasting penetration and revelation of the West's Pandora's box of scientific secrets, but it has as yet denied the prize of liberty, individual freedom and independence of mind and spirit that are the true keys of the kingdom (of Heaven's Mandate on earth).

Be that as it may, the bald facts of the global balance of power are that China's colossal trade surplus with the USA is recycled into a correspondingly massive current account deficit, resulting in a sharp drop in global growth. Making these imbalances more manageable is now entirely in China's gift, as it attempts to boost its domestic market demand.

The three main strands

Of the main strands or components of Chinese power, the three most prominent would appear to be mercantile, military and mental capacity (knowledge and 'intelligence'), and of these three the most important and the strongest is undoubtedly mental capacity. In terms of military might – deployment of land, air and naval forces – China probably has parity with the USA relative to its strategic interests. Its accumulated wall of monetary reserves – and its ability to mobilize these more-or-less to any purpose it wishes – gives it massive economic clout. But the real edge it enjoys, the best weapon in its arsenal for competitive advantage and advancement, is the grasp that the Chinese generally have of Western languages (particularly English) and the insight this gives into habits of mind and Western values. The extraordinary level of cognition this affords of countervailing strategies, empowering technologies and the latest research findings and writings in science, medicine and philosophy – much of which may be painlessly obtained via overseas study and the internet rather than through diplomatic guile and industrial espionage – makes their combination of monetary muscle with wide-ranging knowledge and well-sourced information a powerfully combustible one.

And that power commands the capacity to mobilize 10,000 soldiers for two weeks to clear the sea off Qingdao of algae for the Olympic sailing races – a feat no other country could or would have accomplished. To field such a force is not merely a matter of available manpower. It is an illustration of the remarkable pragmatism of Chinese actions, rooted as they are in a steely resolve to solve physical problems by human means, where mechanical or technological means are unserviceable. This power is also the consummate skill of the archer who draws his bow string back to the point of maximum tension and holds it precisely long enough to loose his arrow with the truest and deadliest aim. These are powers of mind concentrated on the exertion of physical pressure to assert the supremacy of the will. Both examples serve as metaphors for China's alertness and latent military prowess.

By the same token, its current economic clout and power to affect foreign economies is clearly evidenced by its default underwriting of American debt and its fearsome stockpile of foreign exchange reserves, its huge investments in Australia, Africa and Latin America and its ability to acquire key strategic holdings in major multinational corporations. The force of a nation's expansionary and foreign policy is exerted through pressure and physical presence, but its effect can be much reduced and blunted by the extent to which recipients may yield to its impact and parry or absorb its advances. The balance of probability is that China's overtures in these sectors will be more than welcome, particularly in the developing world.

The subtle, lasting spread of a country's power and influence is achieved much more indirectly through the open manifestation of its culture, language and values as attractive forces for change and good in the world. How 'cool' now is Mandarin as a new medium of understanding between different cultures and civilizations, a live channel of discovery to each other's modes of thought and expression, ambitions and pre-occupations? So much more of China's heart and mind that was previously inscrutable is now accessible and intelligible. How revealing of China's spirit of long-suffering and growing sense of individual selfhood in this postmodern world is the sound of its popular music and its vigorous life of action in pursuit of new leisure activities. Music and sport now serve to regenerate the sinews of a delicate morale. Will its food and music, painting and dance, theatre, film and literature, calligraphy and athletic prowess prove sufficiently alluring to woo distant peoples into its recreational fold?

While Russia withdraws into itself, threatening to re-mobilize its colossal firepower to defend and re-assert its interests worldwide, China draws country after country into its web of influence. Through careful cultivation of cultural ties in Asia, Africa and Latin America, and robust championing of the developing world in the face of Western trade hegemony, these fast-evolving relations are cemented with instant working capital, preferential credits, manpower and machinery, and new overseas markets for commodities and manufactured goods. We wonder how deep is the attraction on which these close new relations are founded, and how stable and steadfast a partner China will prove to be. What values are at work here to persuade such disparate societies to make common cause?

With the failure of the Marxist model, China may gain reinvigorated faith in a new ideal of equality and the enabling power of state capitalism to re-order old hierarchies, social orders and ex-colonial dependencies. The current establishment of Confucius Institutes worldwide as the vanguard of China's cultural presence is a token of a new renaissance or reversion to Confucian values as the mainspring of its motivation to expand and control its influence in the world. Some hint of from where this motivation may be derived – apart from the state's concern with alleviating the common scourges of hunger and poverty – is the Chinese individual's sense of moral outrage felt at the injustices and humiliations suffered at the hands of the West in the nineteenth century. Even more keenly felt is the growing awareness of gross inequities in the distribution of wealth, not only in China but also in the economies of many of its formerly impoverished trading and investment partners overseas. Thus the potential for mutual co-operation, based on shared values and a common history of oppression and interference by foreign powers, is clearly appealing.

Western tables are turned

China is now the country of impact from the East, with the West scrabbling to devise an adequate response. The character and spirit of its incursions into faraway places is quite distinct from the course set by Britain and the trading patterns, relations and dependencies it established from the late seventeenth century. Furthermore, it has nothing remotely in common with the *mission civilisatrice* of the French (and Portuguese) in Africa, Asia and Indo-China. Rather, its impetus seems to come purely from pragmatism and the need for procurement of vital resources with no quest for 'dominion over palm and pine' (and the wearisome burden of administration that would clearly result).

But will its peaceful rise via 'soft power' initiatives amount to anything more than soft loans and credit lines, and sporting, cultural and scientific exchanges with other countries? Surely only when China is co-opted fully into the world's councils (the IMF or its successor and the G8 or its successor, as a matter of some urgency) can there be sufficient fusion of international intent and commitment to mind the world's shops and counting houses. In this endeavor, China can count as yet on little leverage from its own non-governmental organizations (NGOs), one of the most essential of the 'soft power' instruments.

The pattern emerging is the projection of a steady assertion of self-confident identity, dignity and fellow-feeling for other very disparate races, backed by the most practical of assistance to poorer countries in the construction of infrastructure and the provision of sundry goods. The benefits that accrue to China from this massive bootstrap operation designed to lift itself and other countries out of poverty are largely monetary – from a straight commercial/barter exchange of overseas resources – rather than genuine goodwill resulting from cultural appeal and attraction. Does this make their Confucius Institutes appear to be Trojan horses?

As we remarked earlier, there is in the Confucian teaching on the ordering and conduct of human relationships (the *wu lun*) no provision for dealing with the stranger or foreigner. Can this human-centered moral code for living with no apparent spiritual or quasi-religious dimension extend to true feelings of benevolence and interdependence with broad humanity, once dislocated from that quintessential sense of place in a homebound community, family descent and honor, and social context that is the defining feature of Chinese identity? The true effectiveness and depth of its influence abroad will only be measured by the extent to which its public diplomacy succeeds in engaging the hearts and minds of the broad masses of the people in those countries in which it invests and seeks to befriend.

Upturned tables but not a flat world is the true perspective. China maintains its walled world of superior wisdom about how it orders its affairs in an international context and its superior knowledge of how other countries are seeking to contain, constrain and curb its influence. There is a mutual perception of arrogance and high-handedness between West and East in particular, which is based largely on base ignorance and irrational fear. The power of the Western democracies is weakening under internal strife. In the UK, parliamentarians are mired in the mud of sleaze and 'slushy' expense accounts. In the USA, the Guantanamo Bay ethical disaster rolls on and on. In Europe, the resurgence of communist political parties is proving attractive to many. As the West struggles, we see the shining mental citadel of Confucian rectitude and forbearance as something of a lodestar for China in the many areas of darkness in Asia, Africa and Latin America. A soft light of benevolence suffusing the spirit of China's giving and receiving?

We can begin to see why China is peculiarly gifted in reaching out to the world for succor rather than dominion. China is not seeking to level life, nor to standardize it across the globe; rather, it reminds the West that life is a struggle and that only by learning, striving and unremitting hard work will humankind advance.

CHAPTER 7

Opportunities

Those who write theory like Confucius never make money.

(Attributed to Mr Wing Yip, Wing Yip Cash & Carry Supermarkets)

Introduction

The global financial crisis of late 2007, 2008 and into 2009, made a dent in China's much-vaunted export earnings and international trade surplus. But it has also provided the spur for China to encourage the growth of its domestic market and to stimulate consumer demand. In truth, this is the real focus for China. It may be first in the world for production of commodities and consumer goods, from cement to tea, but is in the bottom third of the world for income per head of population. This creates a dilemma for Western economists – is China a developed or a developing country? Which set of fanciful definitions and mathematical models can be applied to fathom Chinese progress? In short, none. China is developed along the Eastern and Southern seaboard but developing elsewhere. Western minds cannot handle mutually exclusive situations. China is too big and too diverse to fit neatly into the economic models' premises and parametric boundaries.

It has an average savings rate of 30–40 per cent of income, representing a huge untapped source of investment in the economy. It will become almost an act of faith in China's future and a patriotic duty to loosen the purse-strings and spend more of the household budget on local products and amenities. Green technology will now have much greater scope for development, with China as a test-bed for a new industrial revolution in renewable energy supply and environmental protection with the temporary respite from intense, hell-for-leather manufacturing and industrial activities for export. Outbound China is similarly favored: as its domestic cost base rises, so much of its low-end manufacturing can be relocated abroad, along with its newly created brands, in alliances with international partners. Outbound migration will also follow hard in its wake as more Chinese citizens opt for overseas passports along with their investments as an important diversification of their interests and an insurance for their families and business succession.

The chances for China to take advantage of its strong position in a new world order to extend its influence have never been greater. Its new role as generous benefactor to many poorer countries gives it an almost unparalleled access and presence. Yet there seem to be constraining factors operating to limit the extent of its political influence overseas – not least its aversion to interference or involvement with foreign domestic administration and local government. Thus what is clearly emerging is less a series of alliances based on shared political ideology or principles, and more a series of bridge-heads established in countries with regimes and local elites likely to comply with and acquiesce to China's need and demand for primary resources and commodities in exchange for cash and credits.

These countries in Africa and Latin America feel a certain solidarity and equality with the other, albeit larger country of China, in their mutually developing world. China may be taking opportunities but it is clearly not seeking to colonize them. In its most literal sense, this form of opportunity provides China with its rationale for dealing, transacting and identifying the least expensive control over economic exchange. In this sense, there is much less concern for China over principle and compromise and much more concern with securing supply sources through patient building of economic relationships as linchpins for maintaining and sustaining its mid-to-long-term sphere of influence.

Worldwide expansion for the Chinese brings an exciting new dimension to thinking and acting, accustomed as they are to grasping and capitalizing on shorter-term opportunities for swift advantage and profit in trade and investment. Such adventurism will require a different order of calculation and anticipation of its consequences. The emplacement of Chinese capital, goods and services tips the balance of influence and dependence in their favor and creates an entirely new level, color (inevitably more grey than green) and depth of interdependency between developing nations. It also creates a new order of long-term commitment, both moral and financial, to South-East Asian, African and Latin-American regions of the world. At the same time, the Chinese are systematically buying up shares in Western resource and services companies and mastering the exercise of control over a company with a less than majority stake. The cash customer is king.

Developing and developed traffic

One vast, uncharted area for growth in China's overseas expansion is the provision of aid to poorer countries. This will become a key feature of their public diplomacy over time, but is as yet largely unstructured, sporadic and randomly targeted. Aid freely given to assist another country's development can and does lead to long-term links in education and training, and eventual self-sufficiency. It should never replace the recipient country's resource base or be allowed to become a surrogate umbilical cord for its basic sustenance. It can be tied to large contracts for the provision of infrastructure and the supply of machinery and equipment, but is more truly enabling if it causes a country to acknowledge its cultural affinities with the donor and to share its values. Thus aid programs are extremely hard to implement and implant successfully without the agency of NGOs and their workers on the ground in the recipient countries, and the rigorous supervision and administration of contracts and disbursement of funds to ensure that monies reach their intended destinations and beneficiaries.

NGOs such as the Red Cross/Red Crescent, Oxfam, Action Aid and so on are prime movers in international disaster and hunger relief efforts in thousands of life-saving and community-building initiatives in the developing world, but the real work of channeling government funds and services to poorer countries falls to organizations such as the UK's Crown Agents, which acts as a hub for the radial supply of services to over 110 countries worldwide. These services are comprehensive and include procurement and logistics; health; public finance; consulting; training; engineering; banking and investment; legal advisory; and humanitarian assistance. China will seize the initiative in these areas and gradually become a main supplier and service provider of choice for the developing world.

And in the developed world we see, for example, London full of Chinese opportunists, many of them illegal immigrants, smuggled in for a hefty fee (around US$30,000 raised through family donations and loan sharks) and free to labor unmolested by anyone other than their 'snakehead' gangmasters as they work off their debt. Some work inhuman shifts in Chinese restaurants or takeaways; others peddle counterfeit DVDs on the street; more enterprising souls grow cannabis plants in rented houses with plenty of floor space for their internal greenhouses, which only come to light when helicopter patrols discover that snow has inexplicably disappeared from their roofs in winter!

Almost all of these Chinese gamble and many of them fight, attack, kidnap and kill each other as if there were no law either to stop them or to protect them. They inhabit a world of sweaty insecurity and alienation, fearful of arrest, shuttered away out of sight in miserable lodgings with only floor space for their bedding roll to call their own. But there is evidently gain to be had from the pain of their displacement, which far outweighs the sense of loss and separation from family and familiar culture that has to be endured.

If it were not for the venality and criminality of many of these characters, most could be regarded as mere rascals or even picaresque inhabitants of a *demi-monde* in which no one will admit to having an address and all flit like ghosts around familiar haunts in many different cities. The rewards of such reckless endeavor are the very same as those that loomed so large in the hopes and dreams of their nineteenth-century forebears – those who, once done with the fantasy of 'chasing the dragon' of opium-smoking, escaped to a much harsher reality of gold-mining and railroad-building in the USA, precisely because they had so little to lose. Thus it is that such a mentality persists, one in which the weighing of risk and reward is akin to Wall Street: huge and irrational risk is taken to achieve a gain, while minimal trouble is taken to avoid a loss. The illegal immigrant shares only his risk-taking with Western financiers.

The effects of the West's immigration policies and much compromised asylum law have been aided and abetted by highly organized crime networks from East and South-East Asia, and have encumbered the machinery of justice with an intolerable burden of costs in court cases and trials of those illegal immigrants caught committing murder, kidnap, drug peddling, money laundering and credit card scams. In China, by contrast, as a steady measure of control in 2008, all casual foreign workers – for example, English teachers, Filipino musicians, freelance writers of PR puffs for airlines – had their business visas rescinded, ostensibly to enforce tax payment on their earnings, but in fact to demonstrate the country's effective security system and to protect it from undesirables. Authority and control – but with reason. Imagine the fate of anyone seeking to enter China illegally, even for such innocent purposes!

After the ovations

There was some concern after the Olympic Games in August 2008 that Beijing and the whole Chinese economy would suffer an inevitable slowdown and loss of momentum – the so-called 'Olympic curse' suffered by cities such as Mexico and Montreal. The cost of the Games, estimated to be around US$44 billion, seems astronomical when compared with London's budget for 2012 of under US$20 billion. But in the vast scheme of things that is China's investment programme this is only a drop in the ocean of national expenditure on infrastructure, housing and communications. (Beijing itself accounts for only 3 per cent of national GDP.) Growth fell below 10 per cent in 2008 and conservative estimates for 2009 are just below 8 per cent, off the pace from previous years but reflecting the impact of the global economy on China's performance.

While external demand for China's goods and services is bound to be affected by the 'credit crunch' in the West, the revving of its domestic engine of consumption and new investment will most likely compensate for this relative slowdown in growth. A burgeoning middle class is emerging in China's cities, since more than 30 per cent of young people are attending and graduating from universities. Although spending on cars, computers and air travel is falling off, retail sales are definitely rising in third- and fourth-tier cities and rural markets. While the currency (the renminbi or RMB) is likely to appreciate by 3–4 per cent against the US dollar in 2009, exports that recently accounted for some 40 per cent of GDP (as against 14 per cent for the USA) are set to slide. On the domestic front, investment in fixed assets – chiefly in infrastructure for the inland cities, upgrading of railways, new housing stock, electricity and water supply, environmental protection and clean-up, mass transit systems and the reconstruction of the earthquake-ravaged towns and cities of Sichuan province – will also spur employment and growth.

The net effect of the Olympics' success and the celebration of the Games as a catalyst for protest by disaffected citizens and 'netizens' or bloggers has been to make the government more responsive to people's concerns. There is a greater readiness to listen to and accommodate dissenting views on the thorny issues of land use reform, environmental protection and inadequate medical services raised by NGOs and other pressure groups and activists. Many restrictions have been lifted, particularly on freedom of movement within the country. Press freedom has been sharply curtailed, however – the toxic milk powder scandal of 2008 was kept out of the papers by government embargo on the story through the issue of the Chinese equivalent of 'D' notices – state security injunctions – but information is becoming much more freely available.

With general access to the internet and mobile communications, thought control is quite impracticable. Major sites and sources have been unblocked, including the BBC Chinese service, Amnesty International and Human Rights Watch. However, this apparent relaxation of control is somewhat misleading: of the seventy-seven protest groups who made application to demonstrate during the Olympics period, more than seventy had their complaints resolved through dialogue. The rest were not accounted for, but may have reached their designated stamping ground unreported or more likely been sent for re-education through labor, a common means of dealing with troublemakers, thus by-passing the courts. The most common disputes involve compensation, land holdings, and environmental pollution, damage and degradation.

While business costs rise ineluctably, the incentive for China to consolidate, restructure and move up the value-chain in manufacturing is fast driving change and impelling companies to shift production of low-end goods such as shoes and textiles to countries like Vietnam and Bangladesh. New labour laws, partial unionization and rising wage rates, land, electricity and transport costs all conspire to cut away at productivity and slender profit margins. Additional exacerbation comes from the government's urgent need to address the widening differential in living standards between the inland provinces and the prosperous coastal regions.

The economy slowed over 2008 and 2009 but will forge ahead as domestic demand for goods and services increases. The bogey of inflation with a headline rate of 6–7 per cent in late 2008 has receded to 1 per cent, with a corresponding threat of deflation, though severe drought and resulting foodstuff shortages will continually threaten to raise this figure. Underlying pressures have been strong: price controls are still in force on grain, coal and utilities, which distort the full extent of inflation. But then inflation control is not the top priority. It is growth that is paramount – growth not at all costs, but at the heavy expense (for the time being, at least) of the environment, health and social welfare.

Despite rising economic growth, accompanying freedoms are less substantial. While freedom has made great strides in several areas of Chinese life, such as private business, education and diplomacy, it remains severely restricted in the key areas of information, public broadcasting and press media. Thought control and limitation of public discussion and debate still pervade society. The classical tactic of 'hide–placate–lie' is still commonly used to conceal accidents and unpleasant truths by officials and official organs of communication – radio, TV and newspapers – while apparent achievements in the national economy are given undue prominence. Media coverage is generally partial, bland and tendentious, and certainly not designed to encourage open, public debate of pressing issues and concerns.

Much of this official obfuscation is undermined and bypassed through access to the internet and mobile communications, which provide instantaneous news of events as they happen and a forum for spontaneous discussion through blogs and private causes taken up by activists brave enough to challenge the authorities. Avenues of redress for wrongs and injustices suffered seldom lead anywhere through the courts and it is often left to networked non-government organizations (collectively) and individuals (singly) to pursue their cases at their own expense and in their own time in the face of constant stalling at the lowest levels of petition to officials. Recourse to the law and court hearings for these cases has to be extended beyond the domain of commercial disputes before Chinese citizens feel they are able to obtain equity and justice.

The Great Learning

Overseas education has the greatest attraction for the Chinese. It is seen as the highest value good that can be purchased freely. Even less affluent parents are prepared to pay up to US$3,000 for a one-month preparatory course for the TOEFL (Test of English as a Foreign Language) and SAT (Scholastic Aptitude Test) exams for foreign university entrance. A five-year course is estimated to involve an outlay of some US$250,000. For business people, this is not so much to do with dynastic succession as with giving their offspring an international vision to help globalize their operations.

After thirty years of Reform and Opening, most Chinese who can afford it want the chance for the upcoming generation to breathe the fresh air of competing ideas after the stifling conformity of doctrinaire socialism that they themselves were initially forced to embrace. As long as China persists in advancing socialism and developing a socialist market economy, it will continue to wear a self-imposed straitjacket of confinement in vital areas that require both innovation and a free market system to enable it to grow and prosper.

What tantalizes China is its potential to develop home-grown industries in major high-tech sectors: the automobile industry, to include electric and hybrid cars; telecommunications, to include open-source mobiles and its own 3G communications standard; nanotechnology; health sciences; biotechnology; avionics and space technology; and, of course, acceptance of the efficacy of its traditional medicines and acupuncture to complement and compete with internationally patented pharmaceutical products. So much of this has been achieved in the past through a process of reverse engineering whereby the origination and manufacture of products formerly based on foreign technology has been gradually taken over – as with the semi-conductor industry in Taiwan – enabling companies to move swiftly up the production value-chain.

Not for nothing have the Chinese given priority to science and technology at a time when there are dwindling numbers of Western students in these disciplines. Western education has lost much of its rigour in mathematics, physics, chemistry and languages at both school and university levels. Accusations of a general dumbing down are constant, with Western financial constraints plus global league tables making university education and the overseas degree a pricing, rather than an educational, target for fee-paying students. The Chinese thus seek to consolidate a march already stolen in these competitive areas and to press home their growing advantage in the application of advanced technology and low-cost manufacturing.

The advantage is certainly regional, and as a 'Greater China' slowly coalesces around the Middle Kingdom, the country is acutely aware that the success of its influence and prestige as a nation lies not in hegemonic control or military superiority, but in extending its economic sway over the Asia-Pacific region, particularly the ASEAN countries of Brunei, Cambodia, Indonesia, Laos, Malaysia, Myanmar (Burma), Philippines, Singapore, Thailand and Vietnam. The 1997 Asian financial crisis hastened the acceptance of China's economic assistance, and a sophisticated strategy to envelop the region is clearly emerging: the use of foreign aid to forge firm ties with South-East Asian governments; building extensive networks for co-operation on meeting local development needs; and promoting pro-China feeling and cultural attractiveness through quasi-governmental projects, including tourism.

In the South-East Asia niche, China's foreign aid exceeds that of the USA. The official annual figure is given as around US$1 billion, but the total amount is reckoned to exceed this substantially. CAFTA (the China–ASEAN Free Trade Area) was established to allay fears about brutal competition in export markets for high-end manufactured goods, and China–ASEAN GDP in 2007 was more than US$2 trillion. This illustrates China's determination to orchestrate regional integration. One significant example of bilateral co-operation is the 'eco-city' project devised by Singapore and China to build a model city in Tianjin based on ecological sustainability. Cambodia, Laos and the Philippines have all urged China to invest more heavily in ASEAN countries to shore up their stumbling economies in the wake of the global crisis.

Into Africa and Latin America

In line with its policy of treating all countries equally, China has made deep and rapid incursions into Sub-Saharan Africa, principally as an infrastructure financier. Its financing in this sector totals more than that of the World Bank and the African Development Bank combined. It is particularly sensitive to charges that it is plundering African nations for oil and mineral resources, and behaving like a neo-colonialist in these countries. Indeed, there is some justification in its claiming that these infrastructure commitments are addressing the continent's huge deficit in this area. Its investment was under US$500 million in 2001, US$7.05 billion in 2006 and US$4.5 billion in 2007. Chinese oil imports from Africa are still only 14 per cent of total African exports, compared with 40 per cent to the USA and 17 per cent to Europe. Investment in African oil exploration has been only about US$10 billion as against US$170 billion by the West. The match is a fair one: Africa's urgent need for infrastructure is met by China's globally competitive construction industry. The British colonial dream of a Cape to Cairo highway is at last being fulfilled with the completion of the final unpaved stretches of the Great North Road between Kenya and Ethiopia.

Of equal significance is India's commitment to development projects in Africa, an investment of about US$500 million, likely to rise to US$2 billion soon, and its increased credit lines of over US$5 billion. India's annual trade with Africa has risen to about US$30 billion – it is a major supplier of low-cost technology and generic drugs – while China's is double that, at US$60 billion. In India's favor are its human rights record, its broad use of English and its historical ties with Africa as one of the continent's oldest trading partners, particularly in countries such as Ethiopia, Kenya, Uganda, Tanzania, Mauritius and South Africa. However, China has also made swift inroads into these countries as well as into West Africa and the Red Sea Horn, particularly Sudan. African countries increasingly favour trade and aid deals with these two Asian powers, as they come with fewer strings attached than deals made with the West. Aid commitments by the West of US$25 billion by 2010 have not yet been made good – only 14 per cent had been realized by 2007 – and look to be severely constrained by the global economic crisis.

Relations with Central and South American countries have been developed forcefully by China from the initial impetus provided by Deng Xiaoping's plan to create a model of 'South–South' co-operation in the region. This has been part of an overarching policy designed to seek closer ties with and to champion their fellow developing countries. China's main interests lie in sourcing raw materials and food – from oil and copper to soya beans; developing infrastructure; and selling manufactured goods and technology. For its part, Latin America is keen to attract investment from China as a means of loosening ties with and lessening dependence on the USA. China has now become South America's second- or third-largest trading partner since the late 1990s, and trade volume has risen tenfold to over US$102 billion, already exceeding the original target of US$100 billion by 2010. It rose to US$112 billion in the first three quarters of 2008, up 52 per cent over the same period of 2007.

But this is still only 5–6 per cent of both sides' total trade. Major trading partners are Brazil, Mexico, Argentina, Chile and Peru. Although most Central-American countries maintain diplomatic relations with Taiwan, Costa Rica switched allegiance in 2008 and Cuba still enjoys strong Chinese support. In exchange for the supply of raw materials, China is providing assistance in the development of high-tech industries – in Brazil, for example, it is collaborating in the peaceful use of nuclear energy and in the national space programme. Ties are now further cemented by China's new donor membership of the Inter-American Development Bank (formerly a key vehicle for US influence in the region), where its preliminary contribution of US$350 million is to be invested in the development of micro-enterprises and small and medium enterprises in the continent.

CHAPTER 8

Equilibrium

Two bodies cannot be in equilibrium with another unless
they are also in equilibrium with each other.
                              (Zeroth Law of Thermodynamics)

Introduction

China's race for economic growth has ridden roughshod over mere
mortal concerns for its most precious land, air and water resources.
These resources have been recklessly despoiled in pursuit of an
industrial revolution that has been accomplished in about a third
of the time it took for Europe and the USA. The consequences are
plain, painful and alarming: the widespread scarring and very evident deforestation and desiccation of the land, and contamination
and pollution of the air and water speak much more eloquently
than any statistics of the devastating ravages by man of nature in
China. The dry river beds, the creeping desert rims, the palpable
particulate in the air, 'blue sky' about as frequent as 'blue moon'
are all stark reminders and warnings that these primary resources
are probably finite and not naturally renewable.

This focus on development at the expense of the environment
has also produced many unforeseen consequences in the human
sphere: the mass migrations of people from the inland provinces to
the coastal pockets of prosperity in search of work have resulted in
an unimaginably rapid scale of urbanization, pollution and unrest
as a reaction to harsh living and labor conditions under inadequate
planning, zoning and housing conditions. These conditions have
also given rise to chronic fear and anxiety about illness and accident, since the cost of medical care beyond basic clinic and out-
patient treatment is prohibitive for most people. It is perhaps ironic

that the neighborhood committees that were responsible as their brothers' and sisters' keepers for controlling and monitoring the lives of individuals under the regimes of Chairman Mao and Deng Xiaoping are now charged squarely with helping the poor with work placements, health care and general welfare.

The social safety net – once raised to a level to ensure total security for the individual – has now been lowered to ensure that local communities must fend for themselves with minimal state subsidy. This may, of course, turn out to be the beginning of a grass-roots (democratic) participation and representation in local and regional problem-solving and decision-making for policy formulation at a national level. It must be said, however, that in the midst of this colossal and nerve-racking effort to get by for the mass of the Chinese people, the notion of the 'carbon footprint' is about as remote and sophisticated as the pipedream of a smog-mask fitted with a pure air filter for everyday wear. The vexed question of meeting the cost of combating climate change and reducing carbon emissions may well be used by the Chinese as a bargaining counter or trade-off against the USA giving up or sharing control of the IMF/World Bank.

The main culprit is coal

China has the world's largest production. Its appetite for coal is voracious and insatiable. It fuels the power stations, blast furnaces, factories and winter grates across the country and provides almost 70 per cent of its electricity supply. It also creates some 10 per cent of the world's carbon dioxide (CO_2) emissions at any one time, and kills hundreds of miners a year directly through mine accidents and hundreds of thousands of workers indirectly through lung disease from plant effluents. Decreasing its reliance on coal is clearly one of China's top priorities. How to shift this burden of power supply to nuclear and hydroelectric by 2020 is one of its most pressing challenges. Dams designed to stem the tide of overwhelming annual floodwaters and generate alternative hydroelectric power supply have begun to reduce this overdependence on coal. But these same dams have also changed the course of the Yellow River, causing major irrigation problems where beds run dry, and the Yangtse River's flow is being widely diverted to service the industries of the northern cities that are chronically short of water. Over half the people in China still do not have access to clean drinking water. It remains a developing nation to many and developed to only a few.

Air quality in most cities is so poor that it hastens the death of many people from fatal coronary and respiratory diseases. China has now overtaken the USA as the world's biggest producer of CO_2 emissions from factories and carbon monoxide (CO) from road traffic. Although signed up to the Kyoto Protocol on global warming and climate change, it still does not enforce environmental protection laws and measures, pleading that 'developing countries need room to develop' in the face of US 'hypocrisy' and intransigence. So its CO_2 emissions level remains uncapped, and the will and action to implement environmental protection initiatives is largely left to the 2,000-odd independent environmental NGOs registered with the government rather than to the ministry-level government body charged with this task.

Beijing promised a green Olympics and ordered the forcible relocation and shut-down of factories and replacement of vehicles over the summer period, but these measures can only be seen as stopgap as long as the overall air quality and level of pollution remains unimproved. The clamor of the voices of dissent and protest has been muted by the dust and sparser oxygen of the desert and the city. China sees itself as likely to be hobbled by unnecessary costs and restrictions that will handicap its development and place it at a disadvantage in the balance of power between East and West. It is the closing of this gap in competitive advantage that is China's primary concern.

It is here that we come to the nub or pivotal point of our argument: the environment and energy are bound together inextricably. If any sort of equilibrium is to be achieved, it will only come from further diversification of energy supply sources and far greater use of sustainable forms of renewable energy. At present, barely 7 per cent of China's energy is derived from renewable sources, chiefly hydropower. This portion is set to double by 2020, since China has the greatest hydroelectric capacity in the world, with the Three Gorges Dam the biggest power station of all. Nuclear power accounts for only 2 per cent of electricity generation, though will also double by

2020. The National Action Plan does not set targets for the reduction of CO_2 emissions, but following this plan could reduce greenhouse gases by 1.5 billion tonnes by 2010. One fortuitous, though probably unintended, result of the one-child policy in China is the reduction of CO_2 emissions by an estimated 3 billion tonnes. This hardly counterbalances or offsets by itself the serious social problems resulting from this policy, which we believe will end within a decade.

A selfish equilibrium or a green fuse?

Both the West and China are faced with populations that demand more. China's increasing dependence on costly foreign oil is almost causing the country to mortgage its future. But it is the environmental cost of this dependence that is far heavier. Equilibrium with balanced growth and energy security will only come from alternative renewable sources of supply. As the consumption of fossil fuels as energy sources slowly diminishes, so the alternative forms of renewable energy partially supplant them. Hydropower will provide the bulk of these renewable sources: in 2006, hydroelectric output was 416 billion kilowatts.

Solar power generation is a fledgling industry in China, but the country is still the largest consumer of solar energy, particularly for water heaters (in 30 million houses). Wind power is being harnessed increasingly through offshore turbines and inland farms in the wilder north-eastern regions of the country. Total capacity rose from 2.67 million kilowatts in 2006 to 6.05 million kilowatts in 2007, making China the fifth-largest producer in the world. By 2020, a total 30 million kilowatt capacity is envisaged.

China's Energy Blue Paper from the Chinese Academy of Social Sciences has shown that the average rate of recovery of coal from mines was barely 30 per cent, compared with about 80 per cent in other major coal-mining countries. It also showed that extraction from small-scale mines was inefficient, wasteful and dangerous. If the overall rate of recovery could be doubled, however, then a saving of about 3.5 billion tonnes of coal could be achieved. Energy experts estimate that dependence on coal-fired plants will decline to 30–50 per cent of total consumption. The balance will be met by oil, natural gas, hydro, nuclear and biomass power, and other safer and cleaner renewable energy sources. Coal-to-oil production is the first step in the tortuous shift to energy security. As a further safeguard, the electric power networks of China and Russia may well be linked, so that China may bring in power from Russia's far-eastern region for its north-eastern industrial areas.

The real driver of climate change and global warming is, however, population growth. The world's population by 2020 has been estimated to reach 9 billion. With far fewer children being born as migrants move to cities to live and work, China's contribution to this slowdown is likely to be significant. At the same time, increased production of genetically modified (GM) foods and better control of contagious diseases will further improve the environment. Water shortages will be dealt with partly by diverting rivers and canals and partly by desalination plants on the coast. Mining for fossil fuels and copper deposits will slowly decrease, but only if a geo-political will can be forged to ensure that national interests do not take precedence over global interests.

It is estimated that China needs to strengthen its investment in low-carbon-emitting energy sources by a further US$398 billion, or US$33 billion per year, in order to achieve its 16 per cent alternative energy target of the total energy consumption mix by 2020. Stronger enforcement of environmental policies is already creating an increased demand for low-carbon investment. In present-day, coal-dependent China, renewable energy accounts for only 7.5 per cent of the country's power mix. In 2007, China invested US$12 billion in renewable energy, second only to Germany.

The newly established National Energy Bureau has announced that China will invest more in nuclear power and also tap deeper into hydropower, which is predicted to supply 190 million kilowatts by 2010, up from 117 million kilowatts in 2005. Wind farms are expected to generate 10 million kilowatts by 2010, up from 1.31 kilowatts in 2005. Solar power is predicted to generate 300,000 kilowatts by 2010, up from 70,000 kilowatts in 2005. And by 2010, it is also expected that biofuels will produce 55 million kilowatts, up from 2 million kilowatts in 2005. In 2009, China is likely to become the world's leading exporter of wind turbines, as well as achieving a substantial market share for solar water heaters, home appliances and rechargeable batteries.

Domestic consumer demand, however, will remain low for at least a decade. The gross value of China's domestic market is only US$1 trillion – a fraction of the US consumer size. Economic stimulus is thus aimed at infrastructure and poverty alleviation with US$14.6 billion earmarked for clean energy development. China is thus well on its way to becoming a 'clean, green superpower' and is confidently expected to give a global lead in energy efficiency by 2050 – when nuclear power (25 per cent) and renewable energy (25 per cent) are like to account for over 50 per cent of the country's energy mix. By then, dependence on coal may well have been substantially reduced and on fossil fuel by as much as 50 per cent, with a dramatic impact on air and water quality, the environment, health and social welfare. Current policies such as carbon emissions trading, cutting government subsidies to heavily polluting industries and enforcing environmental protection laws will go a long way towards ensuring the realization of this major global test-bed project. A healthy equilibrium between society and the market place is the goal.

CHAPTER 9

Military

War is an art and is not susceptible to strict formulae.
(Attributed to US General George Patton)

Introduction

The PLA (People's Liberation Army) is the combined army, navy and air force of the People's Republic of China in one unified force. It numbers a total of 7 million – the world's largest standing army of 2.3 million, with a remaining vast reserve of veterans and militia. This figure has, however, been rationalized downwards since the 1980s, and reduced significantly to allow for the funding of economic development. Nevertheless, China still calls on its youth between the ages of 18 and 22 to do two years' national military service, with special dispensation for full-time students, but the latter nevertheless must also report for military training for several weeks a year. Since the 1980s the perceived threat of invasion from Russia has faded and the focus of possible military engagement has shifted from Taiwan (a decrease in the threat of a declaration of independence) to the Spratly Islands (to protect China's claim to sovereignty over potential offshore oilfields). The national military strategy is now to be combat-ready for 'local wars under high-tech conditions', not massive ground fighting. China is happy to let the USA and EU nations focus on the Taliban, on Darfur, and on anti-insurgency. China can imitate these military techniques later. This change in military strategy has pushed the onus of delivery of a rapid response to danger and confrontation on to the navy and air force. Looking further ahead, the PLA is also preparing actively for cyber and space warfare.

Tactical asymmetry and Taiwan

In spite of its numerical superiority, China's military operational capability remains perhaps ten years behind that of the USA in terms of nuclear capacity and parity, communications and deployment of land, sea and air forces. Its main concern, of course, is the eventual integration of Taiwan with the PRC. The US Carrier Strike Group stands ready in the Taiwan Straits to intervene should China attempt to take Taiwan by force. Since China knows that such action by the USA could be decisive, if not ruinous politically, the PLA pursues a strategy of attempting to deny 'battlespace' or of 'anti-access' instead of attempting to confront the USA head-on. Therefore this strategy is known as 'asymmetric'. The inspiration for this approach is straight from China's most famous general, Sun Tzu: 'Supreme excellence consists in breaking the enemy's resistance without fighting.'

In the face of overwhelming technological supremacy, China does not need to control the sea or overcome the enemy, except through diplomacy. The PLA is thus focusing on deterring the entry of the US Fleet's floating sea bases into the Taiwan Strait. Its key weapon is its submarine fleet, which poses a serious threat to US carriers. Some of its nuclear-powered vessels operate underwater for up to forty days and remain undetectable to US surveillance devices. The main strength of the USA is also identified as its main weakness: its integrated network of command, control and communications systems.

The PLA knows that attacking information systems could impair US capabilities much more effectively than conventional armed warfare, and the capability to disrupt the US C41SR network of satellite and telecommunications systems may prove to be a highly potent form of strategic deterrence. The only real defense against such disruption would be for the USA to carry out military exercises without using continuous, high-bandwidth communications between units. As any risk of confrontation on Chinese trade routes raises its head, so the stakes rise for the USA as it contemplates intervention in the event of an attack on or invasion of Taiwan (or anywhere in Asia) by Chinese forces. China has now allied itself with a grouping of several bordering states to form the SCO – the Shanghai Cooperation Organization, which will act as a counterweight to the North Atlantic Treaty Organization (NATO) in maintaining the balance of international power in the Asia-Pacific region. The states forming the SCO include Russia and its former satellites – Kazakhstan, Kyrgyzstan, Tajikistan and Uzbekistan.

The West is already overstretched in its military commitments in Iraq and Afghanistan. Afghanistan will finally put paid to US adventurism in the Middle East and will sound the death knell for US and British intervention in regime change everywhere, just as Vietnam defeated the USA by going underground and fighting to the death to defend its homeland from enemy invasion. The cost levels of these commitments are immense and a day of reckoning is imminent. The USA and the UK face a conflict of endless attrition. With its attention diverted, the USA has lost the chance to resume crucial bilateral military exchanges with China, discontinued after the US spyplane collision with a Chinese fighter in 2001. These were called off after President George W. Bush declared a US$6.5 billion arms sales plan to equip Taiwan, an action that only served to prolong and heighten expensive military tensions. The West has to concede that China and Taiwan must be left to decide their own common future, especially as economic ties continue to strengthen. The Obama administration has a long way to go in correcting past US errors.

The stance of the Chinese military, while combat ready at all times, is therefore primarily defensive. Since the Russians no longer pose a threat, there are no heavily manned garrisons along their shared border; rather the PLA is chiefly deployed to maintain internal security, particularly in the troublesome borderlands of Tibet and Xinjiang, where dissent and insurgency are rife. The Chinese air force is well-equipped with jet fighters, bombers and long-range rockets and missiles, but it is the navy that plays the most crucial role in defending China's territory and disputed claims to islands and oil-fields in the Yellow and South China Seas.

As the level of life improves in China, the government is most concerned about maintaining not just territorial integrity, but also vital Chinese interests at home and abroad. Closest to home is the prospect of an eventual peaceful annexation of Taiwan by the motherland under a Special Administrative Region status, similar to, but more comprehensive and complex than that accorded to

Hong Kong. Abroad, there are vital shipping lanes to be guarded, particularly those used for international trade and the transport of key oil and mineral supplies. There is also China's burgeoning sphere of influence in Africa and South America to be protected. The threat of regional disputes over sovereignty with neighbors should not be underestimated. The Spratly Islands in the South China Sea are claimed by China, the Philippines, Malaysia and by Vietnam for their proximity to possible oil shelves. All these are potential flashpoints for conflict.

Mutually assured destruction and combat readiness

Advances in systems of sophisticated weaponry are rapidly making up the shortfall and technological gap with the USA, since China is sparing no expense in buying in such devices from Russia, Israel and other arms-dealing countries. Apart from its long-range ballistic missile and bomber capability, it is also highly adept at cyber warfare, having invested heavily in command and control computerization for military intelligence, surveillance and reconnaissance. Indeed, it is no exaggeration to acknowledge that US defence and communications systems have been widely penetrated, not just by rogue hackers, but systematically and institutionally by the Chinese government and the PLA. As one US military advisor has commented, 'It's as if they were playing chess and we were playing checkers. The point of check-mate has almost been reached.'

The biggest shift in military preparedness has taken place in the sea. Chinese naval forces will soon be able to count on fleets of aircraft carriers and nuclear submarines, which will be second to none in advanced technological capability. They will also deploy fleets of long-range patrol ships to guide and protect convoys of container and transport vessels through strategic shipping and supply lanes.

Two major military exercises – 'Sharpening' and 'Vanguard' in 2008 – demonstrated that the PLA has developed a comprehensive mechanization and 'informationization' of its weaponry and equipment. This enables it to conduct warfare at a technological parity with all the other nations of the Eurasian landmass. Against the USA, its weapons are a potent mixture of force and psychology:

- Sale of US Treasury Bills, which make up 50 per cent of its foreign exchange reserves invested to underwrite US debt.

- Destruction of US spy/surveillance satellites.

- Cyber warfare – attacks on and break-ins to the computerized nerve centers of US command and control headquarters.

- Thought-control: via censorship/blocking of e-mail traffic and internet content.

The clash between the US Impeccable and Chinese patrol vessels in the South China Sea, early in spring 2009, is not seen as big a flashpoint as the collision between the US EP-3 and the Chinese fighter in 2001 – largely since both sides want to avoid any heightening of tensions at such a fraught time for international negotiations with G20 meetings and the financial crisis so prominent. However, any apparent surveying/intelligence-gathering by the US Navy within the 200 nautical miles of China's coastline (claimed as the extent of China's EEZ – Exclusive Economic Zone) are deemed to be hostile acts by China, if it is not informed beforehand.

The Chinese navy has its biggest submarine base on Hainan Island and with its new aircraft carriers is making the China Sea a main theatre for its 'first island chain defence' line, which includes the Spratlys, the Paracels, the Macclesfield Bank and other small islands that may lie over oilfields. Since China's Asian neighbors also lay claim to these islands, they are a major source of friction and future dispute. China will continue to test President Obama's will and policy resolve – just as they did with George W. Bush in 2001. It is also an assertion of China's power and leading role in an emerging Asian free trade zone – at a time of cautious advance for China and apparent partial retreat for the USA following its departure from its main bases at Subic Bay and Clark Airbase in the Philippines.

But in fact no quantity of sophisticated missile defence shields can be guaranteed to ward off long-range, intercontinental ballistic missile attacks. It seems that psychology and negotiated compromise are ultimately to prevail – as they did in the Cuban crisis of

1963 with the eyeballing brinkmanship of the US/USSR stand-off between Kennedy and Khrushchev. The UK defense and aerospace establishment recently came under sustained cyber hacking attack in 2008 from a China eager to plunder the supposedly rich seams of nuclear technology, policies and battle plans that are embedded in its systems. Even a massive assault such as this can thus far be securely thwarted and resisted. The supreme enemy battle generals still remain not the grand military marshals and commanders but rather General Knowledge and General Intelligence (under the possible leadership of a Chinese General Electric).

The American Sun Tzu

The true all-American hero of our recent age is not 'The Duke' John Wayne, but rather an obscure and highly eccentric and maverick US Air Force Colonel named John Boyd. Boyd's is one of the most truly astounding stories of intellect and will prevailing in the face of official skepticism and indifference. He saw his only active service as a fighter pilot in the last months of the Korean War in 1952, but his keen observation of air combat between MiGs and F-86s in that theatre allowed him to elaborate his 'Energy-Manoeuvrability Theory' of aerial combat and the concept of the 'OODA Loop'. The MiGs were getting the better of the F-86s, when clearly the F-86s were the more agile and maneuverable aircraft. Boyd deduced that the American pilots were seated higher in their cockpits, which marginally hampered their capacity to react and respond to danger and attack compared with the lower-slung Koreans. Thus, the pilot who completed his 'OODA' (Observation-Orientation-Decision-Action) cycle the quickest could shoot down his opponent before the latter was able to complete his cycle of reaction and response.

Boyd wrote no treatise on military strategy and his theories on warfare are confined to a lengthy slide presentation, 'Discourse on Winning and Losing', and a short essay, 'Destruction and Creation' (1976). In this essay, he provides a philosophical basis for his theory, by incorporating Goedel's Incompleteness Theorem, Heisenberg's Uncertainty Principle and The Second Law of Thermodynamics to elucidate the rationale for the OODA Loop. He saw three elements in warfare: Moral – sapping the enemy's will to win through alienation and internal dissension; Mental – skewing his/her sense/perception of reality through propaganda and cutting communication lines; and Physical – obliterating his/her key resources of logistical infrastructure, soldiers and munitions.

He also stretched Darwin's evolution theory to imply that natural selection takes place not only as a matter of biology but also as a social process (survival in warfare or business in open market competition). Thus heightened competition hastens the speed and accuracy of assessment of one's opponent's disposition, which can provide the clinching advantage. His theories were tested to devastating effect in the first Gulf War and in the 'shock and awe' US invasion of Iraq. By this token, and in light of their relentlessly more incisive hacking attempts, it is only a matter of time – unless confrontation can be averted by peaceful means – before the Chinese break into the insider track of the West's 'OODA Loop'. Then we shall see where the Western world has lost its past moral, mental and physical supremacy.

CHAPTER 10

Science

When China, developing the resources of her magnificent domain, and clothing herself with the panoply of modern science, becomes, as she must in the lapse of a century or two, one of the three or four great powers that divide the dominion of the globe, think you that the world will continue to be indifferent to her history?

(W. A. P. Martin, 1886, *Journal of the Peking Oriental Society*, vol. I, p. 135)

Introduction

If the pillars of wisdom in the West are law and religion, then China's great moral and ethical touchstone, as noted earlier, is Confucianism, which guides and governs the norms of behavior in a person-centered world. The primacy of education in China – as a driving value in society – reinforces the old ranking of the social order: scholar/official, farmer, craftsman, trader/financier. However, China's headlong rush towards modernization, economic reform and liberalization has brought about fundamental changes to this order as a pragmatic concession to the new priorities of its domestic and overseas trade and investment policies. With the widening of the bounds of knowledge and curiosity comes demand from its people for a new institutional framework to meet social needs for recourse and redress in an order of civil society in which people participate at the grass-roots of the decision-making process.

The Party's current official watchword and guideline is the concept of 'scientific development', which seeks to achieve an elusive social harmony via 'sustainable development', social welfare and increased democracy. This policy is pursued in the face of an evident lack of basic democratic rights, persistent, endemic corruption and a mounting chorus of carping over the *bujun*, the sense of gross inequity at the widening gap in living standards between the towns and cities and the countryside, and the rising tide of environmental pollution. Although avowedly more populist in approach – with pledges to cut taxes for 700 million farmers and to provide subsidies for rural schoolchildren – this policy, while apparently indicating a social focus and concern for the redeployment of workers laid-off from state-owned enterprises and the country's labor and industrial safety record, will probably not be allowed to impede the course of economic growth and the targets the Party has set for its achievement.

When the Chinese talk of 'scientific development' or a 'scientific outlook on development', what they mean is that they are aiming, like the developed countries over time, for balanced growth and sustainable development – in short, a harmony between humankind and nature. The year 2001 was something of a watershed for China: in that year it succeeded in its bid to host the Olympic Games in 2008; it established the Shanghai Cooperation Organization as an Eastern counterpart of NATO ahead of being accepted by the World Trade Organization as well as launching its Shenzhou II spacecraft as a prelude to the launch of a manned space mission. All these events signalled China's desire and capability to play a major role in international affairs. The country is now the world's largest steel producer and has in recent years launched men into space and a space module to orbit the moon.

However, back at the homestead, all is not so well. The harmony between humankind and nature is proving much more difficult to attain without acknowledging a few brutal truths about the environment. Many problems thought to have been caused by flooding and bad weather, for example, have been shown through scientific enquiry, to have had human causes, or, as one of their scientists put it, 'a revenge of Nature on our neglect of ecology over the years'. This evidence has now been recognized and policies have been reversed to return farmland to woodland, grassland and lakes, and to stop the logging of natural forest on the upper reaches of major rivers.

China resurgent

The national revival that is now well under way and that will be the bedrock of China's overseas expansion is still plagued by several severe problems and challenges. These are chiefly the breakdown of rural ways of life and the need for many more urban workers, giving rise to widening disparities in income and living standards; the creation of a new management and entrepreneurial class in a centrally controlled regime; the new opportunities afforded by overseas study of new ideas and technologies – and the risk that such exposure poses of alienating young Chinese; and the containment of civil unrest arising from cases of government abuse and corruption.

But, as always, these problems are relative when seen in a historical context. In the UK, as a result of the Industrial Revolution, living standards rose by 50 per cent to 75 per cent in a lifetime (then about forty years). Between 1978 (the beginning of Reform and Opening) and 2007, China's real GDP grew at an annual average rate of 9.8 per cent, while per capita GDP rose from 381 RMB to 15,973RMB. Thus, the number of 'dirt poor' people has decreased – from 218 million in 1980 to 23 million in 2007. In addition, up to 70 per cent of poor rural farmers are covered by a cooperative medical insurance network. In Table II.1 we show how China leads the developed world in production and economic size, but also that it is a developing country with very low per capita income.

Income disparity, or the *bujun*, is the single most worrying issue for the government. As an absolute measure of income inequality, China's Gini coefficient – an internationally accepted yardstick of this disparity – is estimated to be 0.47. Any figure over 0.4 is deemed to be 'alarming'. In 2006, the information, computer and software industries offered the highest pay, 4.69 times the income of agricultural workers. The new sectors of the economy, especially services, are fast outstripping the traditional ones. Financial services and scientific and technological research are prime examples of this. Education is seen as the major key to closing the inequality gap, but a real bar to progress in this area is the outdated system of household registration (*hukou*), which separates urban from rural dwellers. Without official residence certificates in large cities, children of migrant workers are denied the right to local schooling beyond junior high school.

Table II.1 China's world-ranked position

Year	1978	2008
Gross domestic product	10	4
Per capita GNI*	175 (188)	132 (209)
Total value of imports and exports	27	3
Volume of production		
Crude steel	5	1
Coal	3	1
Crude petroleum	8	5
Electricity	7	2
Cement	4	1
Cotton fabrics	1	1
Cereals	2	1
Meat	3	1
Seed cotton	2	1
Tea	2	1
Fruits	9	1

*China's position, against the number of countries in the world in brackets
Source: *China Statistical Yearbook* 2008, Appendix 2.6.

Table II.1 shows the duality in China – a leading industrial producer but an impoverished nation for the majority of its people. It is this duality which causes imperfections to arise in many economic models. What then of young people's dreams, values, ambitions and motivations? This generation is the most emancipated of all, the most loved and the most challenged. In the hierarchy of goals, their desires are surprisingly idealistic: equality and harmony in society, helping disadvantaged groups and achieving national prosperity, all rank in equal importance to having good jobs and owning apartments and cars. The spontaneous formation of hundreds of NGOs to take up major public causes is a lively manifestation of this.

It also demonstrates the strong natural tendency towards collective participation in promoting civic awareness of the need to address environmental and social problems in a more proactive way. The Sichuan earthquake in May 2008 was a catalyst in galvanizing co-ordinated action between government, NGOs and ordinary citizens in rescue and relief efforts. Similarly, effective environmental protection will necessitate concerted multi-tasking between local authorities, pressure groups and industrial workers in statutory compliance, energy conservation and technological innovation.

Perhaps the most significant change in the lives of individual Chinese since the late 1990s has been their growing sense of privacy. With economic revolution has come a transformation of the local neighborhood committees or groups of watchdogs and minders who policed the daily lives of citizens as the Party leaders' low-level henchman in the Communist chain of command and the ordering of individual lives. Now strangers, including migrants, are no longer stopped and questioned routinely about their residence and right to travel freely between cities. The one-child policy and domestic arguments are no longer quite so closely monitored.

The whole process of prying into people's private lives has been discontinued in favor of a kind of peripatetic Citizens' Advice Bureau which patrols a neighborhood, dispensing practical assistance with employment, benefits for the poor and disabled, recreational activities such as table tennis and song contests for the elderly, and legal aid. There is now little intervention – unless requested as mediation – in the event of a complaint, for example, about excessive noise by one resident against another. This new order of better qualified committee members is often accompanied by a small army of young volunteers who help to improve living conditions and offer tutoring to poor families for little or no reward.

The post-1980s generation (*balinghou*) is coming into its own in a climate just as challenging in many ways as the one in which their parents grew up. With the speed of change accelerated by market reforms, the pace of life and work is harsh and unremitting for those aged under thirty, who currently account for some 45 per cent of the population. There are higher numbers at university, but fewer jobs available on graduation. A couple's only child is also expected to send the parents money and to look after them in retirement. The Chinese National Committee on Ageing estimates that there will be some 175 million people aged over 60 by 2010, to be cared for by only children. The motivation to learn, work, adapt and play is thus among the fiercest in the world.

Freedom from disease

In the days of the 'barefoot doctors', the rural paramedics trained in Mao's time to minister to the health care needs of the rural poor in China, practically everyone could be assured of eventual medical attention. A generation later there is no such assurance: clinic and hospital visits must be paid for, and these out-of-pocket expenses are often simply beyond people's means, particularly when hefty deposits are required before surgeons will operate – even in emergencies. The gulf and inequality between urban and rural standards of medical treatment has become a contentious point and one of the greatest causes of discontent in the country. Health care can account for up to 50 per cent of household expenses because of unaffordable health insurance.

The average cost of admission to a hospital is almost as much as China's annual per capita income, and more than double the annual income of China's poorest 20 per cent of the population. In rural China, infant mortality has recently been around 120 for every 1,000 live births, compared with around 25 in developed countries. Of 1,000 children born, 64 will not live beyond the age of 5, compared with 10 in the cities. There are simply not enough doctors and trained medical staff to deal with these cases. Even in the cities, there is a preference among medical and health care graduates to seek work with pharmaceutical and biotechnology companies.

In the resulting absence of basic primary care facilities in both cities and village communities, people visit hospitals for all their health problems, which leads to insupportable congestion and heavy caseloads. An additional 500,000 family doctors are needed to meet the kind of ordinary GP services available in Western countries. Doctors and nurses are generally poorly paid, and at present there is no single national body setting qualifying standards or assessing professional competence. Many qualified medics leave the profession to seek better-paid employment elsewhere. The state of disarray in the provision of medical services is currently being addressed by a 'Healthy China 2020' plan, which aims to create a universal health service. In a reversion to the non-profit motive for national health care, the plan envisages a renationalization of the health services in China.

Qing and *Fa*

In Chapter 5 we mentioned, briefly, the concepts of *qing* and *fa*. It is essential to understand these concepts as they reflect the role of law rather than the rule of law in its application to Chinese life and business. Personal conduct and integrity has historically been guided, controlled and determined by the notion of *qing* (loosely, 'feelings, affections, emotions' – as appropriate to particular contexts and circumstances) rather than being circumscribed by legal sanctions under *fa*. In this respect, its order of application is the reverse of the Western approach. This means that business relations are expected to be based on harmonious personal relationships between partners to an agreement or contract. *Qing* has much in common with Western philosophy and the concept of faiths, beliefs and a reasoned basis for intuited conduct, judgement and action.

Even now, it is important to acknowledge that establishing a spirit of trust with potential business partners to a venture at the outset takes pride of place over negotiations towards concluding a contract. Thus, while *fa* – new modern statutes governing and ensuring adherence to strict legal agreements – have been in force since the 1980s, unless the basis of relations entered into is sound, they can quite easily be overturned and overridden by local officials, and frustrated by local administrative regulations.

Confucianism holds that people are naturally good, hence the emphasis on *li*, the prescribed norms of behavior set to prompt feelings of common humanity and shame in dealings with other people. Legalism, the alternative school of thought, which sprang up and evolved at the same time, holds that people are naturally selfish and need to be controlled by harsh laws and sanctions if social order is to be maintained. What is of most significance is that both codes of conduct concede ultimate and absolute authority to a ruler who is above the law.

These two schools of thought prevail and persist today, and this explains much of the ambivalence and tension in the tussle and conflict of ideas about the application of law in the Western sense (as a codified body of regulatory sanctions), which is unlikely ever to be resolved completely. While pragmatic concessions have been made – for example, in the area of commercial law to accommodate international transactions and agreements – the determination of cases in civil and criminal law is still very much the exclusive preserve of the Ministry of Justice and the Party.

In general, the older generation in China holds to the personal values of *qing* and mediation, while the younger recognizes the importance of applicable laws under *fa* as a reliable guide for effective business management, agreements and contracts. Another highly significant difference in Chinese thinking has been the absence – until the concept or notion was introduced from the West – of any idea of *legal rights*. This goes a long way to explaining the Chinese policy and stance on acknowledging the protection of individual human rights. In the Chinese world view, the patriotic and collective duties and responsibilities of the citizen simply take precedence.

The closest Chinese approximation to the notion of the rule of law is the term, *fazhi*, which is more accurately rendered as 'rule by law'. This is something of a last recourse and effectively unenforceable in a system in which the ultimate authority of the rulers may set it aside. In a society where freedom of information is closely curtailed and sensitive facts and statistics are often still labelled 'state secrets', the growing level of protest and unrest provide amply sufficient impetus for reform. On the thirtieth anniversary of the Reform and Opening movement (1978), the necessary measures to deal with dissent and protest legally and through the courts were in place, but as yet have not been enacted, for fear of ceding the initiative on human rights protection to the tribunes of the people, the lawyers.

There is thus a fundamental conflict of interest between the Party – as the guardians of the 'harmonious society' via the Ministry of Public Security, with its arbitrary powers of arrest and detention – and the lawyers who invariably themselves become the object and the issue of any legal proceedings brought on behalf of injured or aggrieved citizens, particularly in human rights cases. In the absence of any independence for the judiciary, which is totally beholden to the Ministry of Justice and the Party, the 'Socialist rule of law' can only mean that the Party's stance on any case or issue is the only right determination or decision and always overrides legal procedure. No wonder people take to the courts only *in extremis* after all attempts at mediation have failed. Without doubt, *guanxi* will prevail over law for the foreseeable future.

Some animals may be more equal than others

With the demise of the SOEs and the agricultural communes, the state's main focus has shifted at the macro level away from the rural farm worker to the wage-earning urban manufacturing and service industry worker, and from labor to capital as the primary factor of production. At the micro level in the countryside, the inequalities of income and living standards between rural and urban populations are thus exacerbated by the shift from labor (farming) to small-scale capital (business ventures) as the prime source of family income. Small businesses have more scope to diversify income sources from additional ventures than labor, which may only diversify via migration.

There are also large disparities in land-rights distribution with the move away from socialist allocation towards granting land use to households that can make the most productive use of it. The combination of collective land ownership and rising land markets, which allows land to change hands, permits family subsistence farming to continue, while giving the more adventurous and enterprising the chance to change the land use to larger-scale commercial farming or other commercial enterprises to benefit from market opportunities.

The *hukou* system, modeled on the Soviet *propiska* (internal passport), continues to be a barrier, stopping China's rural population from settling in cities and denying them the right to basic welfare services there; 800 million rural dwellers are effectively second-class citizens. The system was previously used as an instrument of labor allocation in a centrally planned economy to ensure adequate farm labor for food supply. But now that 300 million extra workers will be needed in manufacturing and service industries, it has clearly outlived its purpose and usefulness. Although reforms are under way and the *hukou* system is gradually being abolished, control is still maintained by strict local entry conditions to any change in household registration.

Certainly, the Cultural Revolution could be said to have knocked morality sideways. As a result, there has developed among its victims and their more wayward children something of a craving for remoralization. The Chinese hanker naturally after community and even spirituality. This is a large part of the healing process of reconciliation with a life in which values have been re-aligned to enable people to cope with new pressures to compete, adjust and learn. It is a harsh environment in which the state is officially atheist and regards the practice of any faith-based religion, if not quite civil disobedience, then certainly as a threat to its authority.

In part, it explains the rapid rise and popularity of the Falun Gong movement and *qi gong* – both of which involve traditional calming breathing techniques – as people struggled to regain their mental balance in the wake of the government's extinguishing of the democracy movement in 1989. Indeed, Falun Gong is now a persecuted cult outlawed in much the same way as the Vatican might declare a particularly controversial ecclesiastical view or teaching heretical. So it is that the ever-pragmatic Chinese, denied the normal channels for free enquiry and debate about the legitimacy of their government, have found a new god in the worship and pursuit of money. There comes to mind in this context the artfully ironic parody by George Orwell in *Keep the Aspidistra Flying* of the famous biblical passage in St Paul's First Letter to the Corinthians about the essence of the human spirit, in which he substitutes the word 'money' for 'love', thus (here as an example is an adaptation of the King James version):

> Though I speak with the tongues of men and of angels, and have not *money*, I am become as a sounding brass, or a tinkling cymbal. And though I have the gift of prophesy, and understand all mysteries … and though I have all faith, so that I could remove mountains, but I have not *money*, I am nothing. And though I bestow all my goods to feed the poor, and though I give my body to be burned, and have not *money*, it profiteth me nothing. *Money* suffereth long, and is kind … endureth all things … And now abideth faith, hope, *money*, these three; but the greatest of these is *money*. (Emphasis added)

But while the market economy encourages people to hurry to reap its benefits, it also discourages them from contemplation and reflection. There are an estimated 130 million Christians in China.

This figure includes not only those officially affiliated but also members of the numerous unofficial house churches that meet in groups of up to twenty-five people to avoid breaking the law on assembly. At a time of precipitous change, these groups clearly enable people to come to terms more easily with the hectic rate of liberalization and technology. The state keeps a wary eye on these gatherings, seeing them as potential seed-beds of organized opposition – to the one-child policy, in particular. At the same time, it seems determined to be 'inclusive', claiming that religious people's knowledge is vital to national prosperity.

Brightest is not always best

In the West, the seeds of regeneration have already been sown. The prime driver of the American Dream can now be traced back clearly to the seventeenth-century Puritan spirit that impelled the early British settlers in their vision of building a 'Kingdom of Heaven on Earth'. That vision was based on little more than their own manual skills and a strong moral sense of the need to promote the collective fortune of the family and the wider group or community above the interests of the individual. In the UK and in much of Western Europe, the Protestant work ethic had a very similar dynamic. Common to both were a focus on excellent organizational skills and the centrality of the craftsman, designer and maker of useful tools and products. In the nineteenth century, this craftsman or maker would become the engineer and manager, as various more complex and intricate technologies evolved and developed to meet the demands of an industrializing society for specialized tools and labour-saving devices. It was these innovative technical skills that sustained the impetus in precision engineering and manufacturing.

The modern spirit of our age of individualism and self-seeking has caused many of the West's best brains to seek to cut corners and forget the higher purpose of the common good by electing to pursue careers in purely financial (rather than civil, mechanical, electrical, chemical or design) engineering and management with insufficient 'domain' or craft knowledge – with predictable consequences. It was the illustrious management writer, Peter Drucker, who justly claimed that far too many people, especially people with great expertise in one area, are contemptuous of knowledge in other areas, or believe that being bright is a substitute for knowledge. The resulting pile-up of material goods and property on offer through credit has caused the entire market system to clog and choke on its own excesses.

Manufacturing has become an accelerated cycle of planned obsolescence for products such as automobiles and washing machines, when what the world needs most is reliable 'consumer durables'; that is, ones that can be repaired at a cost that does not necessitate a replacement purchase and that do not create such wastage and disposal and recycling difficulties. Inevitably, what will cut across this cycle is the periodic breakthrough of disruptive technologies such as the hybrid/electric car and the digital camera. It is the large emerging markets of China and Indonesia and, to a lesser extent, Vietnam and Mexico, that will become the world's principal manufactories for these products in the future. Just as the Aga Khan on behalf of the worldwide *umma* of the Muslims championed Japan as the model of adaptation to Western manufacturing techniques in the 1930s, so today we may acknowledge that Indonesia may soon take a lead on behalf of the Islamic world, demonstrating that it may well be possible to reconcile Islam with democracy. But it is China that will bear the main load of adaptation, innovation and industrial management in the decades to come. That load will no longer be borne cheaply.

Points to ponder

Points

The essence of what China can teach and what can most profitably be learned by the West may be summarized in the following way: beginning with education as preparation for life, the Chinese urge students, above all, to work hard and acquire knowledge to be successful if they want to make money, but chiefly as a means of attaining wisdom and self-respect. The aim of education is thus the rewarding life experience it affords. Too often in the West, the student is taught that the world is an intimidating and dangerous place, full of traps for the unwary, rather than full of opportunities for those who are hard-working and talented.

This tends to foster an attitude to work as something to be resented rather than valued. The Chinese, in general, look beyond the simple boundaries and embrace wholeheartedly a balance of work and life that is holistic and where there are no strict demarcation lines. Their natural competitive instinct leads individuals to seek out occupations and levels of reward commensurate with their talents and abilities.

Ponder

In contrast to China, the West, with less collective social and familial contexts, has a distinct lack of flexibility in the regulatory framework of its business activity, and criminal, civil and contractual legal systems, which conspire to stifle initiative and hold back those who would provide leadership and create real value in any enterprise or business venture. This is chiefly because of employment laws governing recruitment and job termination (all over-protective of individuals' rights) and the high safety net of social security (which is exploited and abused by the unscrupulous and feckless).

The Chinese have learned patience and forbearance and built up a discipline and resilience in the face of setbacks. This guiding system of basic values enables the Chinese to withstand economic downturns and to recover and respond with greater readiness once an opportunity occurs.

At their core, the Chinese believe in their fundamental difference from the rest of the world as a superior civilization. This belief is based upon neither insupportable arrogance nor some vain and perverse hubris, but upon their calm and certain knowledge and experience of striving to survive and prevail in the face of constant, strict, authority and unpredictable natural disasters. The tumultuous trials and tribulations of successive regimes – from the First Emperor's unification drive to Mao Zedong's Cultural Revolution – have annealed and tempered their spirit. The agony and long-suffering that they have so stoically and painfully borne could in any other civilization have been unendurable.

There is a debate currently raging between Western authors with different perspectives on China and its place in the world. The debate focuses on China's supposed grand design on the world and is largely academic, since the courses proposed for China's development are based upon Western prescriptions. China's own position is clear: it wishes to and will determine its own destiny. Claims advanced by Enlightenment proponents like Will Hutton (author of *The Writing on the Wall*) make no allowance for the fact that China developed its own rational values through Confucius and his successors two millennia ago. These values are so deeply embedded in the Chinese psyche that no amount of Western persuasion and example will ever supervene or supplant them. Indeed, one of the problems with Hutton's argument is that he assumes some set of universal values apparently rooted in Rome and Ancient Greece. Why should Chinese values have roots in the West?

As for the world domination thesis propounded by Martin Jacques (author of *When China Rules the World*), the idea that the West is competing with China in a new modern age is also difficult to grasp. In our view, the West basically competes internally and presently allies itself with China as the downstream producer of cheap consumer goods. Jacques does make the important point that the Chinese view themselves as a civilization rather than simply as a nation. We agree with this perspective as Chinese characteristics are recognized in business research throughout Asian nations.

Daniel Bell, on the other hand, writes revealingly about the modern Chinese world viewed through the eyes of a Confucianist (in his book *China's New Confucianism*). We agree with much of his worldview but believe it is perhaps difficult to align it with Western thinking. Without first-hand experience it is well nigh impossible to see ourselves as others see us.

Finally, we should all take heed of the extremely well-researched work by Jenny Clegg (*China's Global Strategy*). Her book provides an interesting projection of the dangers of a US-led unipolar world. She anticipates a multipolar world with China as a necessary counterbalance to US hegemony. However, we feel that any equilibrium for China is more likely achieved through a dual polarity with the US – a G2 in the making. Nevertheless, it is difficult to avoid her main argument – that critics of China often do not engage in a serious fashion with its modern reality. China's history, its size, its internal development needs, its external positioning and its international image are essential and integrated elements of Chinese government polity and must also be viewed by the West in their related entirety.

PART III

Potential, outcomes, evolution, mastery, second sight

Better fifty years of Cathay than a cycle of EU?
(With apologies to Alfred Lord Tennyson)

Introduction

China is already the world's third-largest economy after the USA and Japan, and the third-largest trading nation, but is still ranked only in the hundredth position regarding per capita GDP. In 2009, it may yet achieve up to 17 per cent of manufacturing output worldwide as against the US figure of 16 per cent. (This is a jump from only 3 per cent in the 1980s.) Given China's prowess in production in the period before nineteenth-century industrialization, this latest surge would appear to justify forecasts of more than a 30 per cent share of manufacturing output by 2025. Three hundred million more agricultural workers will be absorbed into the manufacturing and services sectors, as farming is gradually mechanized. Thus the upside-down world of the Mao era is now reversed, with rural peasants who were previously accorded the highest class rank being shorn of their status and subsidies, and the 'stinking intellectuals' (the lowest) reinstated.

Major Chinese brands such as Tsingtao beer, Lenovo (computers), Haier (white goods), Yili (dairy products and ice cream), Hua Wei (telecoms) and the Bank of China are gaining increased exposure in the global marketplace. All this new-found commercial prowess is being achieved on the back of a giant tidal wave of foreign currency reserves which accrues by the US$ billions with each month. Since the RMB was unpegged from the US dollar in 2005, it has floated slowly upwards, eroding some of China's natural exchange rate advantage. Unwanted hot money flows into China constantly alert the government to the need to manage the exchange mechanism carefully to allow for eventual free exchange of the RMB towards a more equitable international balance of payments.

China's aim in all these efforts is not, contrary to Western belief, to seek some sort of vainglorious world dominance through brutal competition and the spread of its trade, investment and cultural influence at home and abroad. It is, rather more prosaically and realistically, to raise the level of life in China for two-thirds of its people from bare subsistence and joblessness to self-sufficiency and relative prosperity in a single generation – something only partially achieved over sixty years in Victorian Britain.

The Chinese Communist Party is not a revolutionary socialist party at all. It is nothing of the kind. It is not even a political party. It is an unelected and unrepresentative cabal of traditional groupings from the Confucian elites in China with a pragmatic leavening of campaign-hardened peasant veterans to give it some legitimacy and the common touch as the country's governing body. It is rather as if the country were run by an institution like the British civil service, but with executive powers and with workers' participation in decision-making and voting on major issues, not unlike the German *Mitbestimmung* (or workers having a director's seat at board meetings of China Inc.). With the demise of Marxism and class struggle as the great drivers of revolutionary change, China is fast righting the inverted social pyramid of the Mao era and restoring an order of meritocratic governance.

This 'meritocracy' is nothing other than the old system of selecting by examination those fittest to administer justly the business of government. This exam may now begin to resemble 'Modern Greats' rather than to test knowledge exclusively of the Confucian classics. Papers may include questions on politics, philosophy and economics, world history and foreign languages. This system is arguably China's greatest contribution to political civilization, with its emphasis on fairness, competition 'open to all the talents', and promotion based on continuous evaluation of performance in office.

In terms of accountability to citizens, it has proved in the past to be no less effective than electoral democracy. In its devising there has been a constant preoccupation with good parenting (a projection the other way of ancestor worship) rather than paternalism (and notions of George Orwell's 'Big Brother'). Chris Patten used to quote this paradox when he was the Governor of Hong Kong: India, for all its democratically elected leaders, is apt to abuse its people when it finds their dissent inconvenient, while China's unelected government looks after peoples' welfare like parents. More poignantly, Taiwan's democratically elected Democratic Progressive Party government, in power since 2000, has proved to be the most corrupt of recent Asian regimes and set back the cause of democracy on the island by its willful abuse of office. Democracy, even in the West, is challenged by its practitioners. Before the Second World War, the British prime minister, Stanley Baldwin, argued that a democracy was two years behind a dictatorship. Western voter-focused democracy may soon be a decade behind China's parental imperialism.

Metamorphosis

Meanwhile, China's economic model is morphing into a new pragmatic paradigm with freedom of movement in the labor and commodity markets, and rapid deregulation in the freedom of movement of capital across borders. At the same time, Taiwan's experience and example serves China well, as its government intervenes decisively in land reform and usage, and in the direction of the use of its natural resources. The state also has no compunction about using state-owned enterprises, banks and research institutes as public service institutions to enhance both domestic and overseas competitiveness. In China, this is relatively easy to achieve, since, first, there has never been such separation of state powers – between executive, legislative and judicial – as there has in the West; and, second, because neither has there existed such a divide between the state and society as in the West. The two are so much more tightly enmeshed as to permit much faster consensus and action. This is because Chinese social consciousness is focused unerringly on an integration of common interests, both practically and ideologically, towards the ideal crystallized by the British poet, Alexander Pope:

> For forms of government let fools contest;
> Whate'er is best administer'd is best.

The bedrock strength of China's economy as an engine of growth and regeneration lies not so much with its much-vaunted foreign exchange reserves of over US$2 trillion in early 2009 as with its individual housekeeping habits. While Western economies have been driven by consumer debt, Chinese private debt accounts for barely 14 per cent of GDP, compared with 140–180 per cent in the West. Similarly, at the level of the Exchequer, the UK's public debt now exceeds 50 per cent of GDP, while China's is only 18 per cent. The massive stimulus given by investment of some US$600 billion in the infrastructure development of China's second- and third-tier cities will hasten the creation of a vast domestic consumer market made up of a rising middle class with increasing disposable incomes. This will go a long way towards righting, over time, the balance of an economy skewed in favor of, and over-dependent on, exports. If inflation can be controlled, then China may still look to growth rates above the *ba bao* ('save eight' – an 8 per cent growth rate) figure needed to sustain the economy and public order. Notwithstanding the government's faith in this figure, grave doubts remain as to whether the stimulus package will sufficiently incentivize China's ultra-careful consumers to spend more. Even now, after the government has set up national health insurance and pension schemes, the problem is still a rigidly institutional one: as one concerned citizen is quoted by the China News Service, 'It's not that Chinese consumers don't want to spend. We just don't have money, because we need to pay school fees for our kids and foot our relatives' medical bills.'

Political reforms will be slower in coming. China has suffered repeated false dawns in the proclamation of a new order for the country – from the 1911 revolution to Mao's 'New China' in 1949 – and is now faced with an urgent need to ease political restrictions if the economy is to be allowed to flourish as it must in order to sustain its people. *Storming the Citadel: a post-17th Party Congress Research Report* (2007), appeared to contain proposals officially sanctioned (i.e. publication was approved by the Party) for improving the constituent membership of the National Peoples' Congress (parliament), the independence of the judiciary and greater public accountability from the administration.

However, the document does not really address the primary concerns of citizens set out in *Charter 08*, a political manifesto and petition presented by over 7,000 influential opinion-leaders, agitating for change and liberalization. The Party prefers to deal with such dissent and unrest with palliatives such as the provision of universal health care and other repairs to the social safety net, and seems more determined than ever to bring about economic reform without loosening its grip on the reins of political power. This is, of course, a recipe for festering disaffection by the people who enjoy a widening consciousness of China's place in the world. Civic movements such as *weiquan* (literally, 'looking after rights') are increasingly vociferous about abuses of power against numerous victims of Party callousness, indifference and injustice.

The boil must at some point be lanced, but by whom? If not the by the Party itself, then who will step forward with a sterile instrument? The pace of progress toward reform is sporadically arrested and kept in check by a Party that seeks to curb and contain the forces of nationalism and populism. Control of the media and censorship, and spying on the internet and e-mails is justified by the Party as a means of reducing disquiet and anxiety at a time of momentous and unsettling social change. However, once the economy is no longer quite so dependent on exports, China will have less incentive to maintain the status quo in the Asia-Pacific region. China will then be well-equipped to pursue a higher-risk and more adventurous foreign policy without endangering its economic prosperity. That foreign policy adventure may begin with a gamble on North Korea or Burma – partial reform of either or both of these cruel regimes will demonstrate that China is no longer to be treated as a champion of rogue states but as a nation capable of defusing world tension and contributing to global stability.

Executive summary

This final part of our book alerts the West to the likely impact on geo-politics and economics of China's expansion and investment overseas. It also stresses the importance of China's locomotive role in shunting the world economy back on track.

1. *Potential* demonstrates how the 'struggling giant' is becoming ever more agile in its *modus operandi* – not inclined to align itself with Western systemic norms and rules. China is determined to chart its own successful course for development with a resurgence of rational Confucian spirit underlying its one-party rule.

2. *Outcomes* are our views of the results of China's careful new investment and diplomacy, and show how the advances and anomalies of its policies and rising regional hegemony will lead to a steady increase in Chinese migration to invest, live and work overseas.

3. *Evolution* looks at the heart of the common causes of combating global warming and achieving renewable energy sourcing and interracial harmonies.

4. *Mastery* details some of the emotive historical events that have spurred China to restore itself to a central place in world affairs, protect its widening sphere of influence and join the exploration of space as an equal partner.

5. *Second sight* prefigures some key features and drivers of China's twenty-first-century advancement in politics, education, moral and spiritual life. It welcomes the integration of China into a much more active presence and participation in international affairs.

Finally, we summarize our argument and await the arrival of an exciting new epoch.

CHAPTER 11

Potential

Know then thyself, presume not God to scan;
The proper study of mankind is Man.
(Alexander Pope, *Know Thyself*)

Introduction

The challenge for the West is to reconcile its value systems of democratic rule and fundamental freedoms of movement, speech, expression and assembly with China's monolithic, authoritarian and collectivist one-party rule and its Confucian heritage – but not to try to impose them. In this equation, there is an essential difference in the notion and quality of freedom: the Chinese sense of self is much more closely bound up with family obligation and pride in the standing of the nation. The Westerner is more concerned with the extent of individual autonomy: as the American philosopher, John Dewey, says, 'What men actually cherish under the name of freedom is that power of varied and flexible growth, of change and disposition of character, that springs from intelligent choice.'

Confucian tradition still underpins a patriarchal and hierarchical society in China, and the ordering of individual lives within it. Thus advancement and life choices are clearly circumscribed by the notion that respect, power, prestige, rank and reward should be accorded to people as they meet criteria that are ethically relevant to their needs and capacities. The world, turned upside-down by Mao Zedong, is gradually righting itself with a reversion to education being the principal means of advancement in a natural meritocracy. This is a meritocracy of ethical achievement, which adheres to a gold standard of peer-approved fitness for office. Thus its authority derives from the deference shown (and demanded by) people in official positions. The Confucian spirit is essentially autocratic and authoritarian. It does not expect to have to justify orders and to explain reasons to people. It demands a deference to educated officials, who are deemed to know what is best for people. In the face of non-compliance, the natural response is to use coercion.

This Confucian spirit does not encourage discussion, debate or people's participation other than through formal communication based on mutual dependence, trust and commitment to shared goals, meaning and understanding. In his *Analects*, Confucius is effectively silent on any such notion or identifiable concept of freedom. The most we can deduce from his writings is that true freedom comes only with maturity and responsibility, and is only really able to be exercised over the age of seventy from the rich store of wisdom and knowledge that ought by then to have been acquired. It is certainly not to be entrusted to unformed individuals. China's current reappraisal of its past is leading to some restoration of this Confucian spirit in the consolidation of its bureaucratic controls. These are being reinforced to preserve norms of governance and to provide protection from the interference of external (particularly religious) influence and authority. This reflects the Chinese cultural legacy and preoccupation with *li* or rules of ethical conduct, which deem virtue, integrity and the promotion of social harmony to be of far greater importance than money-making, and the ancient disdain for trade and capital accumulation.

There is a Western school of thought which holds that China's Enlightenment has in some way been delayed. In fact, China's Age of Reason began well over 2,000 years ago, with the benevolent, human-centred philosophy of Confucius being officially adopted by the state. The Chinese have always dwelt on the civil side of life as being more important than the military, and on diplomacy and powers of dissuasion as the most effective military strategies. These values of treating other states are as valid today as they were two millennia ago.

The roots of Chinese philosophy and thought lie largely with their *li*, their rites and proper rules of conduct, devised and codified by Lao-tzu, the Old Master and keeper of the archives in the State of Lu around 500 BC. Confucius, who worked with Lao-tzu as a young official, elaborated (as did Meng-tzu, Mencius to Western ears, and Chuang-tzu later) his teachings on harmonious family relations, and on virtuous and benevolent rule by kings and emperors. The ideal of society was set as one in which only able people may be elected as leaders, and care and compassion are extended from one family to another. Harmony and diversity were encouraged in order to prevent wars and conflict. States were to treat each other as equals for mutual benefit. In the fourteen years to 484 BC, Confucius is reputed to have visited most of the warring states of China. In 485 BC, then in his fifties, he returned to the state of Lu (modern-day Shandong Province) to teach students, and gathered more than 3,000 disciples in his lifetime. What he taught them, chiefly, was that personal life was more important than fame and worldly success, and that the cultivation of the self towards knowledge, physical and moral strength, wisdom, benevolence and trust was the supreme purpose of living.

His teaching comprised instruction in six basic disciplines:

- *Li*, or the rites or proper rules of conduct.

- Mathematics.

- Calligraphy.

- Archery.

- Charioteering.

- The five books (or classics of literature):

  ○ the *Yi Jing* ('Book of Changes'), a symbol system used to divine order in events;

  ○ the Book of Poetry;

  ○ the Book of Rites;

  ○ the Book of Music; and

  ○ the Book of Spring and Autumn Annals, a history of the state of Lu.

This regime of instruction with its emphasis on rigorous study and physical fitness was eventually found to be so efficacious in the production of competent officials and administrators that by 134 BC it was formally adopted as the official teaching of the state.

The disciples of Confucius set down his teachings in the *Analects*, which resemble the dialogues of Socrates in their pithy and enigmatic aphorisms and epigrams. The body of literary works that have become classics of Confucianism include, most famously, the so-called *Four Books*:

- *The Great Learning* – a chapter of the Book of Rites.

- *The Doctrine of the Mean* – another chapter from the Book of Rites.

- The *Analects* of Confucius.

- The *Mencius* – dialogues between Meng-tzu and state rulers.

The Great Learning stresses the ideal of harmony between rulers and ruled, to be attained in seven stages: the investigation of things; the completion of knowledge; the sincerity of thought; the rectifying of the heart; the cultivation of the person; the regulation of the family; and, finally, the government of the state.

But it is *The Doctrine of the Mean* (Moderation) or *Chung Yung*, that seems to have the greatest resonance today. Again, it contains that negative injunction, 'What you don't like having done to you, don't do to others.' But it also contains, most significantly, the only rule laid down for dealing with foreigners, which can be summarized as prescribing indulgent treatment of them from a distance. However, this refers strictly only to guests, officials and merchants from other provinces. On treatment of other nations, Confucius is silent, because he had little knowledge of people from beyond his borders. But this principle of indulgence has long been extended to cover them too as a matter of expediency.

The *Analects* of Confucius set out the dialogues between Confucius and his disciples, in which he describes the ideal of the superior or exemplary man to which they should all aspire. The essence of his teaching is revealed when a disciple asks him for one word to serve him as a practical rule in his life and Confucius says, 'Is not reciprocity such a word? What you don't want done to you, don't do to others' (Book XV, xxiii). This, of course, is the one injunction that chimes most closely with Christian teaching in dealing with human relations. The *Mencius* is a further collection of disquisitions on the need for benevolence, righteousness, propriety and knowledge by Meng-tzu.

The magisterial Reverend Doctor James Legge, the first Professor of Chinese at Oxford University, was none too prescient when he waspishly averred in the late nineteenth century, 'Of the earth earthy, China was sure to go to pieces when it came into collision with a Christianly-civilized power. Its sage had left it no preservative or restorative elements against such a case.' The irony today is that its sage has left it precisely that.

Shifting the gears in the West, China and India

The summer and autumn of 2008 brought about a singular watershed in world affairs. First, the failure and breakdown of the Doha Round of WTO trade negotiations, and then the precipitate banking and financial crisis in the West signaled the need for real change and realignment in a new world order. The rapid ascent of emerging economies such as China and India and those of the Middle East heralded a new era of globalization, one in which these new powers are ready to challenge the old rules of world trade and finance. These rules were previously set by the USA and the EU, and were more-or-less imposed on lesser countries. Now power is ebbing from America and Europe and shifting swiftly to these newly-emerging economies, whose sovereign interests are of primary concern. China's total trade volume and value is now greater than America's for the first time. India's and China's foreign exchange reserves are mountainous trade and investment war-chests for the acquisition of strategic assets via sovereign wealth funds, private equity and hedge funds, whose opacity strikes suspicion and fear into the hearts of developed countries everywhere. They are widely perceived as a political threat to the control of ports, national assets and financial institutions worldwide. In the vital energy sector, the national oil companies of China, the Gulf and Venezuela have been supplanting the Western oil industry giants, the Seven Sisters, for some time.

All these shifts in the global power balance call clearly for new forums and frameworks for discussion and regulation of this new world order. Major emerging economies such as China no longer wish for nor see the need to follow the rules laid down by international organizations, and agreements such as the IMF/World Bank, G8 and the Kyoto Protocol on climate change. They see these organizations as dealing with issues of interest to the core industrialized countries and therefore do not wish to share the costs. Trade protectionism stalks international talks like an invisible specter. As long as America, Japan and Europe maintain their agricultural subsidies, high import duties and intellectual property rights agreements, global trade cannot be further liberalized, unless a new set of common free trade rules can be formulated and agreed on. In Africa, China's incursions have aroused alarm in the West. Sino-African relations have settled into an aid-and-barter trade pattern that is much more to Africa's liking than assistance from the IMF with its onerous conditionalities having the effect of belittling many countries to the status of 'remittance men'.

In the Asia-Pacific region, the main organizations and forums for wider regional discussion and co-operation were established in 1997 in response to the Asian financial crisis of that year. A formula known as '10 + 3' was initiated whereby ASEAN (the Association of South-East Asian Nations) and the leaders of China, Japan and South Korea met to devise collective actions to avoid future crises and to reduce the cost of regional development and further economic and financial risks. It has since expanded to cover foreign trade, services, culture, education and security. Annual East-Asian summits since 2005 have seen Australia, New Zealand and India join in closer co-operation throughout the region. Japan and Korea have formed free trade agreements with Mexico, Chile and the USA.

In 2007, the USA mooted a cross-Pacific free trade area to restore East-Asian regional cooperation to the framework of APEC (the Asia-Pacific Economic Cooperation forum). These initiatives, together with the Asia–Europe series of annual meetings, provide a working network of correspondence and collaboration that goes some way toward limiting the unforeseen damage to trade and investment relations, but not nearly far enough in providing an international institutional framework for the regulation of governments' behavior. Organizations such as the IMF/World Bank, the WTO and for negotiations like the Kyoto Protocol meetings need to be reconstituted to involve China, Japan, India, Russia, the Middle East and Brazil to address and meet the pressing new issues and priorities of a realigned world order – and to be vested with the authority to make decisions binding on nations internationally.

The near-catastrophe of subprime lending has pitched the USA headlong into its gravest financial crisis since the Depression of the 1930s and shattered share markets worldwide. From October 2007 to June 2008 the total value of shares in fifty major markets sank by US$10 trillion – a 17 per cent drop. Markets in strategic commodities such as grain and mineral resources suffered a similar contraction. To date, it would appear that the WTO is the only organization with the mechanisms to spread multilateral trade benefits and liberalization around the world.

Matching current realities will require a much more robust network of regional groupings to ensure sufficient regulation of trade and investment, particularly for the CRIMB (China, Russia, India, Middle East and Brazil) countries as hubs and their immediate spheres of influence. For the moment, the old G7 plus 1 may have proposed, but the new G20 will dispose as they please. With India and China to the fore, a cursory study of India's potential for future growth and development compared with China's would seem to indicate that, over time, India will have the edge. India has the institutional legacy of the British Raj to build on: its greater literacy in the English language, including a mastery of English nuances and advocacy, and the rule of law. There is a drawback to this: the Indian tends to rely on rhetoric to win an argument, a tactic which fails when translation into Chinese (or any other language) is required.

India's population will rapidly equal China's and its middle class of consumers is currently more numerous. However, these advantages are not all that they seem, and appearances can be quite misleading. The real dynamos for growth have developed almost as unforeseen, accidental consequences of state non-intervention. They are, in India, the IT-based service sector, and in China, the thousands of non-state SMEs in manufacturing and services for export that sprang up spontaneously after the government's abandonment of collective farming. While reform and trade liberalization replaced planning in both China and India, China has been much bolder in its commitment to new investment in infrastructure and communications. In addition, foreign direct investment from overseas Chinese has had a much greater reinforcing role in strengthening capital markets than it has in India.

Indian society is still hidebound by its caste system which limits access to universities and jobs and stunts social mobility, even for the better-educated, while China is avowedly meritocratic, with open opportunities 'for all the talents'. India remains a much more hierarchical society and one that clings more faithfully to socialist values, while China has moved from the egalitarianism of uniform salaries to the pragmatic leveraging of capitalism as a means of raising its people en masse from poverty into prosperity. Ideology is dispensed with in favor of the advance of the nation-state through entrepreneurial endeavor, while India has yet to address the much needed privatization of its nationalized industries. In the wider world, however, India may claim to have stolen a march in entrepreneurial activities in the USA and Europe. China may be catching up fast, but what will separate the two countries eventually is more likely to be their respective institutional capacities to deliver sufficient financial and policy initiatives to sustain their long-term growth. The potential, however, for upward mobility in society rests with China and the Chinese way of doing things.

If we examine certain concrete facts and factors of Indian and Chinese reality, it quickly becomes apparent that some common bases of comparison are on shifting sands and even contain category errors. The most significant is the link, first, between a country's public administration and its decision-making and implementation. In India, this is diffuse, given the nature of its coalition politics, and leads to conflict and delay, whereas in China it is 'top down' and leads to the swift execution of new policies. Second, relations between the different states and provinces in India and China have quite different dynamics – fractious and conflictual in India because of power imbalances between the thrusting South and the more influential North, and more easily aligned in China because of effective decentralization and the lead given by SMEs and township and village enterprises to entrepreneurial development.

Third, relations between government and business in India are based on entrepreneurial aggression, while in China the state dominates and decrees, being 'government as business'. Fourth, the relationship of government to civil society in India depends on accountability to voters, whereas in China it is primarily about patronage of the workers and the preservation of urban working-class interests. Finally, while India maintains the rule of law via its overburdened and often inaccessible judiciary, bogged down with procedural delays and the weight of precedent and case law, China maintains order – with little or no recourse to law, and no independent adjudication other than via negotiation between technocrats and Party members.

The true nature of growth

The individual savings rate in India is around 28 per cent of income, while in China it is more like 40 per cent. The other major significant difference is that Indian saving is mainly for consumption, whereas in China it is mainly for investment, chiefly in new businesses and infrastructure (see Table III.1).

India has a chronic shortage of funding for investment in contrast to China's plentiful supply. India is chiefly service sector-led, while China is manufacturing-led. Urbanization is slow in India – only 30 per cent of people live in cities, while in China it is almost 50 per cent. Literacy in India is about 62 per cent; in China about 74 per cent. Life expectancy is about 64 in India; in China about 75. Access to electricity is about 55 per cent in India; in China it is almost universal. Physical communications are also poor in India with more highly concentrated investment in rural roads only to see them crumble away in monsoons, whereas China is upgrading the quality of both rural and urban roads to an equivalent standard.

A tentative conclusion as to the likely progress of growth in both countries based on this evidence and that in Table III.1 is that future governance will be the deciding factor. India has to contend with populism, crony capitalism and the challenge of promoting

Table III.1 India versus China

Total GDP (2008)	India US$1.2 trillion	China US$4.2 trillion
Investment as percentage of GDP	39%	44%
Consumption as a percentage of GDP	55%	40%
Infrastructure/investment percentage of GDP	6%	8.5%

Sources: CIA, *The World Factbook*; *The Economist* (18.6.09); *Xinhua/China Daily* (26.5.09); *Reuters* (24.6.09); *India Govt* (29.5.09).

inclusiveness in a caste-ridden society, while China has to maintain the delicate balance between harnessing nationalism while not causing its people to revolt because of undue repression and overbearing state capitalism. While India must continue to improve delivery of public services to its poorest to head off the potential of its 'million mutinies', China must continue to give its disenfranchised rural poor more voice in decisions affecting their basic livelihood.

Perhaps the greatest step towards averting conflict in relations between India and China is that from being each other's twentieth largest trading partner, they have now become each other's third or fourth largest. Asia's new beltways run by seething manufacturing and service metropolises – Mumbai and Bangalore, Chongqing and Guangzhou – while in the West the specter of the rust bucket haunts Detroit, Pittsburgh and Stuttgart, Lille and Liverpool.

State capitalism

For all its much-vaunted trade surpluses, foreign exchange market (forex) reserves and sovereign wealth funds, China's main engines of employment remain its heavily loss-making SOEs, which continue to drain and distort its economy. A certain perverse rationale for their existence and maintenance is captured in this comment from a British businessman resident in China:

> As the fiasco unfolds in the United States, I cannot help thinking of the terrifying mantra we have read so often in the past ten years, 'The Chinese banking system is technically bankrupt. The banks have been directed to lend on a political basis to state-owned industries who realistically would find it difficult ever to repay.' That may not be a good situation, but how much better to lend to a failing SOE that keeps 10,000 people employed and lubricating the real economy than to lend to each other on the basis of packaged debt instruments that do nothing but grow in phoney value, enriching bankers along the way but achieving little else. I think the Chinese way may be proved right – completely by accident!

Of the US$200 billion earmarked as sovereign wealth funds for CIC (China Investment Corporation) to invest in suitable holdings to conserve and enhance China's national patrimony worldwide, some US$70 billion will likely be spent on recapitalizing Chinese banks. Some of the balance has already gone into holdings in Blackstone of the USA and in Barclays Bank of the UK, both of which have lost value sharply. These moves, coupled with an increased investment in US Treasury Bonds just ahead of the credit crunch of 2007, have aroused the ire of ordinary Chinese, who feel that their country's hard-earned resources have been squandered. But, from a political standpoint, the June 2009 indication that China will purchase US$50 billion of IMF bonds is perhaps the strongest indication yet of the desire by China to make an international play, not for mere recognition, but for an element of control – an element that appeals to national stability.

All this indicates greater caution on the part of China's overseas fund investors into a Western capitalist system that confers risk but not control, which is just as well, since levels of anxiety have been rising swiftly in the international community over the prospect of predatory raids by China and others on distressed foreign institutions, companies and assets. Sovereign wealth funds have now agreed to table basic operating principles that will respect national regulatory systems: political accountability; clear objectives on maximizing long-term returns; and transparency. Probably more than organizations such as World News Corporation or that past icon of US capitalism – Enron!

Despite the hobbling effect that SOEs have had on the Chinese economy, they have nevertheless managed to nurture and test-bed a substantial number of entrepreneurial ventures, which now form a growing non-state or private sector of the economy. After all, where else could early entrepreneurs have learnt their technical and managerial skills, supplemented by periods of overseas study and research? The transition from a planned to a market economy could not have been accomplished without them.

Companies such as Lenovo, Haier, Huawei and TCL all had their roots in the manufacturing sector of SOEs and have all contributed rapidly to import substitution for a growing middle-class consumer market. Lenovo is now the third-largest PC maker in the world, having bought IBM's business for US$1.75 billion. Later arrivals on the world stage have emerged in the service sector: Alibaba (the international internet trade mart) and Baidu (the Chinese Google) have already had a substantial impact on trade and communications in dealing with China. These later types of company have also been more adept in tapping into overseas capital markets for overseas listings and acquisitions for international expansion.

Another major feature of almost all of these ventures is that their ownership, control and financing has been maintained and exercised from outside China. This is the case for the food company, Wahaha, and for Galanz, the microwave makers. They thus retain a privileged flexibility of operation and benefit at the same time from state encouragement as market leaders. In this way, the state/private distinction is invariably blurred in the interest of what works best for China. Huawei, their leading international IT and telecoms group is the prime example of the special status thus conferred.

The balance of China's US$2 trillion in foreign exchange reserves is being actively managed to make direct investments in the West through its network of major commercial banks, and to encourage overseas mergers and acquisitions in strategic sectors. At the same time, many cash-starved European companies are now being forced to restructure for fear of a takeover by predatory hedge funds and private equity firms. Bank of China is expanding and now targeting the UK consumer with housing loans and mortgages.

Sovereign wealth funds

It is estimated that Asian sovereign wealth funds will grow from US$4.6 trillion to more than US$7 trillion by 2013. Of this figure, the lion's share is held by China, Japan and India. China's chosen instrument is CIC (China Investment Corporation), whose starting capital was set at only US$200 billion. After initial purchases of Blackstone and Morgan Stanley shares, the fund has pulled in its horns in after heavy losses on its holdings in the wake of the global financial crisis and stock market collapse in the during 2008. There has been much recrimination by both officials and ordinary people in China about risky and speculative dealings in the West. Attitudes and operating philosophies have hardened toward treating the funds as national endowment vehicles for conserving core reserves of China's patrimony with much reduced exposure to hedge funds and private equity investment. To this end, more foreign portfolio managers are likely to be employed to ensure the equitable spread of international holdings. In short, the watchword throughout 2008 and 2009 was 'prudence' above all else.

Guo Xijing, president of China Investment Corporation, has remarked that the West had better be nice to China if it wants to win any of its money in sovereign wealth investment. National 'beauty parades' are bound to be fiercely competitive. China's fund is currently one of the world's largest after Abu Dhabi, Singapore and Norway.

The global crisis has narrowed China's options in trying to achieve in a few years what Japan, Korea and Taiwan have taken several decades to do. Its ambition to 'go global' has been transformed into an imperative. It clearly has the financial resources, but it also has a huge amount of ground to make up in management knowledge, capacity for technological innovation, and recognition of its product and brand quality. In a Deutsche Bank report on China's overseas direct investment (by Andreas Lunding, and entitled *Global Champions in Waiting*), China's strategy has moved 'from the political objective-centered to the commercial interest-oriented, from the central government dominated to enterprise-led and from emphasis on natural resource seeking to a focus on resource market and technology seeking investment'. In other words, the worldwide quest has begun in earnest for those 'starter cartridges' of technical knowledge that will fire the vital innovations in product development needed to achieve their economic goals.

In addition to the four major state banks, the other major contenders for overseas ventures are the State Grid, China Food Group, China Life, Baosteel, SAIC (the Shanghai automobile manufacturer), and the 'Three Sisters' state oil companies: China National Petroleum Corporation (CNPC), Sinopec, and the China National Offshore Oil Corporation (CNOOC). While SOEs will still be the main chosen instruments for securing resources and supplies of energy and raw materials for Chinese production, it is the private (non-state) companies that will have to meet the greatest challenges in scouring world markets to expand their brand acceptance through alliances, joint venture and outright acquisitions of foreign companies for their marketing and distribution channels.

Chinalco (Aluminium Corporation of China), the country's largest mining company, is now blocked from raising its stake in Rio Tinto

Zinc by US$19.5 billion, seeking an 18 per cent share. Yet Wuhan Steel, China's third-largest steelmaker, managed to agree a 50 per cent stake in Centrex Metals for iron ore projects in Australia; and Shenzen Zhongjin bought 50 per cent of Peralya Ltd, an Australian zinc and lead mining company. With recovery possible toward the end of the year, 2009 is seeing more aggressive overseas expansion into mining and resources. Outbound activity is picking up as currencies and commodity prices fall and set off more adventurous deals.

There are two main systemic and cultural gulfs that will need to be bridged if these endeavors are to succeed. The first major area of concern is the wide differential in salary scales between Western and Chinese companies. This has much to do with the rating of labor as a factor of production in a capitalist system and it is quite conceivable that pragmatic collaboration between Western and Chinese interests and the straitened scale of the world economy will do much to close this gap. The second area is rather more problematic: the wide disparity in values; that is, the very different understanding of and approach to the need for corporate governance, ethical standards, procedures, compliance, disclosure, reporting standards and accountability.

These necessary new relationships will thus be difficult to order and maintain, given that the signs are that China only really wants intellectual property rights and technology from its investments in order to ship production back home. Most of those long-experienced in partnerships and joint ventures with the Chinese are highly ambivalent in their view of prospects for effective fusion of the respective cultures' operations. One long-term veteran of joint operations was less than sanguine:

> Let me puncture a few myths. First, *guanxi*. You have to build up your own network and trust. It'll take you at least five years. You must have a Chinese partner – both commercially and socially. Then there's the 'knowledge gap'. If anything, it's growing wider rather than closing. Nothing gets properly communicated here. It's the language – it's too difficult and ambiguous … China's growth is bound to level off. The *renminbi* will be forced up along with energy prices and transport … I don't think China will ever integrate into the world.

The 'Liberal Internationalists' are just losing out to the 'Nationalists' in government. They don't see the danger of isolationism, of misreading the world. At the moment, they think they can trade manufactures for financial services expertise. They don't want to pay for it. There's a chronic lack of mid-level business skills in management, planning and marketing, so joint ventures all fail. Only WOFEs [wholly-owned foreign enterprises] work. In any case, very few people actually do business (directly) with the Chinese. Almost all of them simply supply parts and support service to the multinationals and exporters.

One man's urbane, qualified take on the scene is another's nonsense.

CHAPTER 12

Outcomes

To restore a broken culture [is like trying] to repair a torn spider's web with our fingers.

(Ludwig Wittgenstein,
Philosophical Investigations, 1953)

Introduction

The year 2008 was a truly momentous one for China, and events and developments during the year prefigured the shape and character of the likely impact of its growth on the wider world. First, its response to crippling snowfalls over the Chinese New Year showed up painful inadequacies in its national road and rail networks, which prevented millions from returning home for their annual holiday. Then in May a devastating earthquake shattered much of Sichuan Province, killing hundreds of children as they sat in shoddily constructed school buildings. Bloody riots in Tibet exposed China's major sore spot to the world, and then international protests marred their Olympic torch relay around the world before the triumphant and matchless success of the Games themselves in Beijing, crowned by China's first spacewalk on its Shenzhou 7 earth orbital mission.

Just as the 1953 conquest of Mount Everest (or *Zhumulangma,* the 'Saint Mother', as the Chinese call it) coincided with the coronation of Queen Elizabeth II, so the Chinese celebrated the Olympic year of 2008 by relaying the Olympic torch to the summit. The year 2008 also brought in galvanizing legislation such as the Law on the Circular Economy, ensuring the conservation of water and other precious resources and their vital recycling, plus land reformation and redesignated usage to promote economies of scale and enterprise, and a more productive rural economy.

The prospect of unemployment and under-employment for migrant farm workers unable to find work in the cities is currently the most pressing threat to stability and public order in the country. Serious initiatives were introduced towards achieving real environmental protection and a green revolution by raising the Environment Agency to the status of a ministry. Renewable energy sources now include the adoption of hydro, nuclear, coal-seam gas, biomass, wind, solar and wave power, and US$200 billion was set aside for investment in their development up to 2020, by which time 15 per cent of total energy needs should be met from renewable sources, while 28 per cent of national electricity generation should be provided by hydro power by 2015, substantially reducing dependence on the current major polluter – coal.

Finally, the colossal 2008 infrastructure package of US$600 billion announced at the end of the year (and the revival of provincial projects worth another US$1 trillion) committed the country to keep up the momentum of its growth and help to restore stability to the global economy. These are all indications of a country vigorously on the march towards self-improvement, keen to learn from and rectify mistakes, and to face, as Premier Wen Jiabao has stated, 'the intertwining challenges of finance, energy and food' as the basic staples of a common human diet.

The Cold War ranged capitalism against communism to the verge of mutually assured destruction, but by the early 1980s China had effectively withdrawn from this contest, leaving the desperate wrangling over nuclear proliferation and ratcheting of tensions to the USA and the USSR. It had embarked on a new path of economic development, moving increasingly towards a capitalist/ market model out of pure pragmatism rather than any ideology. The communists believed that history was on their side. The capitalists believed that history had, once and for all, resolved itself into liberal democracy with the failure and collapse of communism in the Soviet Union. History has now dramatically changed since the Chinese have clawed back the initiative and at the time of writing are in a position to steer the agenda for the rest of the world and to resume their lost central place in international affairs.

Bothersome borderlands

In the run-up to the 2008 Olympics, the West seized on China's sensitive areas in vain attempts to embarrass the Chinese Communist Party into negotiating with the Dalai Lama, the world's leading Buddhist, over the standing of Tibet and his continued exile in India. At issue were alleged human rights abuses by the Chinese and the denial of sovereignty to the Tibetan people. Tibet has long been acknowledged as an integral part of China from the days of its administration by the Yuan Dynasty in the thirteenth century. Since then, a deliberate ambiguity has been maintained, a kind of default position whereby China has held sovereignty, while Tibetans have exercised autonomy in the region – hence the somewhat euphemistic title used by the Chinese of 'Tibetan Autonomous Region'. The Indians, for their part, are less concerned about settlement of boundary/border disputes (still unresolved) than about security issues, especially with Pakistan, as China is such a heavy presence in neighboring territory.

The nub of the problem seems to be Chinese heavy-handedness in not sufficiently respecting Tibetan culture, while imposing Chinese law and language, restricting Buddhist practices and treating the Tibetans as a 'singing/dancing' minority people rather than as equal partners in the development of the region. The Dalai Lama has claimed that he does not seek independence. As most scholars and constitutional lawyers agree, even if China were to collapse, Tibet would never be recognized as an independent state.

Might China not therefore take a leaf from the well-thumbed British book on forging a multi-race and multi-faith community towards that elusive 'harmonious society'? The matter is of sufficient concern to China, who desires that efforts to develop Tibet be understood and appreciated, such as to warrant the cancellation of the EU–China Summit in late 2008. This was purely in protest at the Dalai Lama's audience with President Sarkozy of France.

While Tibet has become China's hardened underbelly, Xinjiang, its most westerly province (formerly Chinese Turkestan) is its most troublesome and exposed flank. The Uighur people who inhabit the region are of Turkic origin and predominantly Muslim. They have long agitated against China's forced domination of their culture and language, and the resettlement of ethnic Han people into their territory. Like the Tibetans, they feel that their way of life is slowly being obliterated by the Chinese, with scant regard for their minority rights and customs. Whereas Tibetans protest peacefully, as in Burma, through the civil disobedience of their Buddhist monks, Xinjiang's Uighurs have organized an armed separatist movement that carries out sporadic attacks on police stations and other totemic symbols of Party control. Xinjiang will remain a potential flashpoint for conflict unless the Chinese can provide sufficient assurance of regional investment and equal employment for its ethnic inhabitants. In some respects, the West already participates in this. China has developed the port of Gwadar in Pakistan's south to link with the Karakorum highway in the north. If the West fails in Afghanistan and Pakistan, then China is threatened in Xinjiang.

The vexed question of Taiwan's status in the international community is altogether different. The island is inalienably part of the Chinese empire and has been part of Fujian Province since the time of the Manchus. The dispute over its current standing lies at the heart of the struggle between the parallel communist and nationalist revolutions that have yet to run their course. The present regime in Taiwan are the successors to the defeated side in China's civil war, which raged through the 1930s to the late 1940s, when General Chiang Kai-shek decamped and retreated with his forces to the island. Both the CCP and the KMT lay claim to sovereignty over Taiwan, but the situation is doubly vexed by the fact that each side lacks a clear legitimacy to make this claim.

Resolution of the conflict can only come with an eventual convergence of national interests and an accommodation of the renegade province within the framework of China's plans for democratization. At the time of writing, this is very much a two-speed process, with Taiwan racing ahead and China inching towards it, dragging its dead weight of disenfranchised peasantry. A popular line in China is that Taiwan only embarked on democracy because it felt threatened by China and thought such a political stance would give it more protection through solidarity with the West, particularly the USA. This has no basis in reality. In fact, Taiwan's present position is squarely based on the legacy of Sun Yat-sen, the instigator of the 1911 revolution and founding father of the new republic, and his 'three principles' of democracy, nationalism and peoples' livelihood, as interpreted by the KMT, which has always claimed the moral, as opposed to the patriotic, high ground in its struggle with the Party. Its policy is 'No independence, no unification, no use of force and no state-to-state relations' (that is, linked only as economic entities).

After much imaginative stretching of semantics to cover the most improbable eventualities, low-key, unofficial talks between the two sides have resulted in direct air and shipping links, cross-strait investment, direct mail, double taxation and food safety agreements, and protection of intellectual property rights. Apart from the direct transport links that encourage business and promote two-way tourism, there is now substantive agreement on harmonization of industrial codes for the operation of telecommunications, and broad deregulation of the financial services sector. Of most significance is the lifting of restrictions on investment in mainland companies and the repatriation of Taiwanese companies from China to list their shares on the Taiwan stock exchange as a means of raising more capital and enhancing their global competitiveness.

This is all part of an overall plan to make Taiwan a regional operations center for globalizing companies that have hitherto been dependent on Singapore or Bangkok for their fund-raising. Such a *rapprochement* and relaxation of tensions between China and Taiwan will lead inevitably to a heightened sense of security and a corresponding reduction in military spending. Perhaps the most interesting prospect to emerge from this cooling of tensions across the Taiwan Straits is the idea of a Greater China common market or free trading area and customs union conceived as a prelude to closer economic relations.

The USA and the EU, by contrast, are severely hampered in the expansion of their markets, both domestic and overseas, by an acute shortage of credit. The EU also faces the prospect of carrying the cost of its premature expansion from fifteen to twenty-seven member states plus a potential bail-out of its former Eastern Bloc members and their citizens, who will threaten migration westwards in search of work. The Russian threat of further energy supply disruption as well as territorial control in Ukraine, Georgia and the Caucasus is no less worrying now than in 1939.

The diaspora of desperation

China not only exports manufactured goods; it also exports people. Globalization has many guises, and one of its most evident is migration. For impoverished Chinese people with dwindling hopes of employment, this is a traditional passage to a better life. In this context, terms such as 'assisted passage' and 'economic migrant' take on new and entirely ironic meanings, as the assistance given by people smugglers who arrange this far from safe passage to the West comes at extortionate cost, and the economic justification for the move has nothing to do with skills or investment capacity. Many of the young people who arrive in the UK, for example, by the 'underground railway' over the Eurasian landmass immediately exploit the loopholes provided by asylum law, having false identity documents or having deliberately destroyed their real ones. One classic dodge is to claim that they are under 18, which entitles them to state benefits, having once been given leave to remain by default as they are technically stateless. This is doubly ironic, since those Chinese who may genuinely seek to claim asylum to escape religious or political persecution are never able to leave China.

The *Chester Chronicle* newspaper of August 1, 2008 ran a fairly typical example of opportunist activity. It reported that a Chinese illegal immigrant had been cleared of a charge related to cannabis. The defendant said that he had been paid £700 for ten days' work at a house, which involved 'decorating' and watering the plants twice a day. But suspicion had been aroused by his blacking out of the windows and creating holes for ventilation ducts and wiring to power heat lamps. He had claimed that he thought the lamps were merely for lighting and then admitted that he knew he was growing plants in secret circumstances. He had said that if he had known that it was illegal, he would have run away, as he was not a gardener, but a builder. He had been sentenced to nine months' imprisonment – minus 67 days on remand – for possession of false identity documents, for which he had admitted paying £100. Thus is such a tangled web woven with little pretence at practice to deceive.

There is, of course, a rational, humane and compelling case for granting these unfortunates some kind of amnesty and allowing them to stay and work legally for a limited time – say, up to three years – rather than jailing and then deporting them, only for them to return again with more false identity documents. As long as their entry to the UK continues to be facilitated by organized crime at a tariff of around £30,000, they will remain at the mercy of, and intimidation and exploitation by, 'snakehead' gangmasters who regard them as their creatures or chattels until their loans are paid off in full. In the meantime, ferocious turf wars rage over illegal Chinese street hawkers selling counterfeit merchandise. The sale of DVDs and CDs is a pirate market so highly and professionally organized that it deprives the legitimate industry of approximately £500 million in lost revenue each year.

The street value of 'moonshine' cannabis is similarly eye-widening. By far the most costly and socially expensive activity for the UK government is the administration of justice in trying and jailing those caught perpetrating credit card scams, money laundering schemes and kidnapping, rape and murder, invariably preying on their own communities in the commission of these crimes. To permit illegal immigrants to remain to work for a limited period would defray a substantial portion of this current expense by contributing some £1 billion in national insurance and tax payments. It would also remove the present 'Catch 22' bind, under which the granting of the very human rights they seek in recognition of their status would result in their deportation and then into a further vicious circle of deceit, danger and unbearable burden for both individuals and the legal system.

The Greater China bloc coalesces

China escaped relatively unscathed from the 2008 financial meltdown, chastened as it had been by the Asian financial crisis in 1997. It avoided getting caught up in the toxic debt purchases that engulfed the Western banking system and thus suffered none of the acute insolvency and liquidity problems that affected so many big-name financial institutions. The bellwether indicator of a country's economic health in this context is probably the relative amount of debt-financed consumption. In the USA between 1998 and 2008 this amount rose from 62 per cent to 72 per cent (consumption as a percentage of GDP). China's corresponding figure is a much smaller portion of that. China has not only been a mighty producer but also a substantial saver. This has meant that there has even been a relative decline in Chinese consumption over this period.

China's greatest challenge, therefore, is to increase consumption as a percentage of GDP without debt financing by expanding its domestic market and promoting the rise of a consumer middle class. With its foreign exchange reserves, its fiscal stimulus package for the economy and its low gearing/borrowing for both companies and households, it stands to benefit in the mid-term after the short-term headwinds of downturn and contraction have blown over. With domestic growth as its major economic priority, China also stands to benefit from the lion's share of foreign direct investment in the coming years. With the investing world currently downgrading stocks, the global pattern of capital and investment flows is bound to turn in China's favor as a viable and highly attractive alternative. Both Hong Kong's and Taiwan's recoveries will be delayed: Hong Kong's because of its dependence on the volume of trade, which will be severely reduced in the short-term, and Taiwan's because exports represented 64 per cent of its GDP in 2008 (91 per cent of which is technology, chiefly semi-conductors). Taiwan, however, has the great structural advantage of becoming part of China economically (if not politically), with its basic manufactures for assembly in China, its direct shipments and flights to mainland destinations and the gradual expediting of closer economic relations.

One major advantage of this structure is its taxation. No haven of avoidance but one of compliance – to the penalty, not the process. Asian people love flexibility, challenge, opportunity, but detest regulation and red tape. Paying the fine, the tax penalty, is simpler and less burdensome than form-filling. The governments play their part: 'We don't care what you file; this is what we think you should pay' is a common refrain. This is where the West is lost. The accountant for the rich Westerner ends up in negotiation with revenue authorities who cannot afford to sort through the maze of trusts and Caribbean companies. For the general Western taxpayer, there is a threat of conviction if a few dollars more in the pocket is suspected, but not for the financier. He or she will have negotiated a deal, not so much a fine as a contractual absolution from being fined.

Tax has played its part in the downfall of Western capitalism. As a brief example – a company is worth US$100 million and generates cash/profit of US$5 million (forget accountancy tricks of depreciation and so on). It pays 20 per cent corporate tax and its Western government collects US$1 million. Now the smart financier puts up US$5 million and borrows US$95 million (at an interest rate of 3 per cent) to buy the company. Earnings are still US$ 5million but US$2.85 million is interest on the debt and is tax deductible. So the government charges 20 per cent on profit of US$2.15 million and collects only US$430,000. Meanwhile the financier earns 80 per cent of cash US$2.15 million, thus pocketing US$1.72 million. However, his earnings are then lent to other companies to refinance projects at low interest rates and are not taxed until maturity. At maturity, he sells the company and is charged only 10 per cent on capital gains – thus paying a lower taxable earnings rate (capital rather than income) than the cleaner who cleans his office (on a 23 per cent tax rate of income). The UK Treasury Select Committee looked into this and felt it was not what the regulations were designed to do but that was how they worked (roughly). Poor cleaner, impoverished taxpayer, rich financier!

Is it any surprise then that the West is at a loss to help their poorest members of society. The convoluted rules mean that the smart financier can outwit the elected politicians every time. India has the largest tax book in the world (a remnant of the British Raj) followed by the UK, the USA and the EU nations. Until the complexity and inflexibility of Western taxation is dealt with, there will be little benefit to Western governments. The public sector will swallow more and more of the decreasing private-sector tax that is collected. The Greater China/ASEAN nexus is thus shaping up to become a leading power bloc in the world. Its flexibility and enterprise will rival and overtake the West as a main hub of economic activity. The benefits of the world's largest free trade area will feed into education, cultural diversity and world power. And the West will wonder what went wrong.

CHAPTER 13

Evolution

In the struggle for survival, the fittest win out at the expense of their rivals because they succeed in adapting themselves best to their environment.
(Charles Darwin, *The Origin of Species;* see British Natural History Museum, *Darwin Diary*, 2009)

Introduction

The evolving prospects for green revolution in China are decidedly promising. Its frantic search for a balance in its use of energy resources is driven not least by its fear and concern over basic food security and food price inflation as a result of drought, industrial contamination, and transport and fuel costs. A key indicator of commitment and intent is the Chinese auto development project in Shanghai. General Motors, having invested more than US$1 billion in hydrogen fuel-cell electric cars, is collaborating to produce a car for the Chinese market. Motivation to diversify and adopt alternative cleaner energies, such as hydro, nuclear, coal-seam gas, biomass, wind, solar, wave and other renewables could hardly be stronger. The environmental activities of China are being watched closely overseas – the UK All Party Parliamentary committee met in mid-2009 specifically to discuss the greening of China.

For all their mighty investment in the development of alternative energy sources, the Chinese cannot ensure a sufficient renewable supply of the one scarce element that is vital to their survival: water. Drought and lack of rainfall have persistently affected the main rice-growing provinces of Hubei, Hunan, Sichuan and Yunnan, and threaten the summer harvests. At the same time, serious water pollution in urban and industrial areas jeopardizes the supply of clean water for drinking, cooking and washing. Agriculture accounts for 65 per cent of water use, but waste in irrigation means that only 45 per cent goes on crops. The current water recycling rate is 40 per cent, against 75–80 per cent in the West. Both of the country's major rivers – the Yellow River and the Yangtse – have been diverted to supply industrial areas and irrigate farmland. Cloud-seeding rockets are routinely fired to induce precipitation, but these produce little more than the proverbial drop in the bucket.

The headwaters of three of the longest Asian rivers rise in China, so it is small wonder that the country is so preoccupied with its territorial integrity. The sources of the Mekong and the Yangtse are high in the Tibetan plateau, and the Brahmaputra also rises in the Tibetan Himalayas. Access to and control of water supply is thus a pressing national concern. Seawater desalination plants are not really a feasible partial solution, as they are fired by coal, which would make their operation somewhat counter-productive. By 2030, when China's population is estimated to be around 1.6 billion, water resources will most likely have been drained even further. Uneven distribution of resources is also a major problem. Areas south of the Yangtse (about one-third of the country) enjoy 80 per cent of total resources, while north of the Yangtse (the remaining two-thirds of the country) have access to only 20 per cent. Over-exploitation of underground water or ancient aquifers has caused subsidence and further parching of the soil. All these conservancy measures of storage, diversion and pumping will require massive new investment if they are to meet the demands of China's burgeoning population. Could it be that once again the Russians will come to the rescue?

Earth Enterprise

All scientists agree that the Earth's primary source of energy is from the sun. The sun powers the Earth and the energy it radiates is sufficient to sustain light and life on the planet. However, it seems that human beings have not kept time with the pulse of the universe. We have sown and we have reaped ahead of natural cycles. We have produced and we have consumed to excess and to exhaustion. We are stripping the Earth's crust of its fossil fuels and now face a barren future, unless we can learn to better harness, conserve and renew our primary sources of energy. We also need to learn this lesson once and for all: energy equates to finance – that is, the true currency is energy, joules and kilowatts not US dollars, euros or RMB.

However, as any physicist will tell you, the two propositions, time equals money and energy equals finance, are incompatible and incommensurable. This is at root the cause of present human anguish. In our race to compete and consume we have squandered non-renewable resources, laid waste to great tracts of land and caused the earth to overheat and undergo dramatic and dangerous climatic changes. Solar energy is our basic income, with fossil fuel our main supply of capital (likely to last only another thirty years or so) together with those formed from photosynthesis. Our fixed assets on the balance sheet are nuclear fissionable and fusionable elements and other energy sources such as hydro, wind, wave, tide and geothermal. Thus the key issue is this distinction between the different building blocks of the currency we have to spend and save: income and liquid capital plus fixed assets.

If we pursue this analogy of science as a business, then a business model can be based on familiar concepts in physics and the life sciences, expressed in three axioms:

(i)   Energy exists and fulfills the business function of finance;

(ii) Matter exists and fulfills the business function of materials and production; and

(iii) A framework of reference exists for the interaction of energy and matter in the universe, in which the dimensions of space and time can be allocated to two 'operating divisions' – premises and distribution.

While premises is conceived as the space or territory required to generate change in energy, it is distribution through time that is key to our current health and survival, because it is into these areas of city and countryside that energy and energy's waste is widely diffused and channeled. These areas are, of course, what we have come to call the environment.

It is the aim of the Earth Enterprise project to get us all to subscribe to the norm of energy conservation as stakeholders and shareholders in the survival of the planet. Now the world looks to China with its love of nature, and the Chinese intuitive sense of living in balance and harmony with it, to provide the test bed and proving ground for all the necessary large-scale conservation measures to ensure this.

Elective affinities

Charles Darwin's theory of evolution has as its full title *On the Origin of Species by Means of Natural Selection or the Preservation of the Favoured Races in the Struggle for Survival*. This claim that only the fittest are designed to survive contends, in its use of the term 'favoured races', that we are all – humans, animals, birds and fish – descended from a common ancestor. It also contends that the theory of the evolution of all living beings depends on four primary factors: natural selection, variation, inheritance and time. It also depends on one indispensable condition: the ability to adapt to different environments. Thus, as the scientist says, 'theories develop laws and explain facts', which are by no means fixed and immutable. Cultures, like markets, do not collide; they mutate in response to external stimuli.

Change within China has come about historically as a result of contact with and adjustment to foreign invaders and interlopers – Genghis Khan, the Mongols, the Manchus, the European powers in the nineteenth century, and finally Sun Yat-sen (via Hawaii, Hong Kong and the UK), and the Japanese in the twentieth century. More significantly, the rivers of the different human races have run to confluence relatively later with the Chinese, largely because China was not essentially a maritime nation. The overland route from Europe and Central Asia – the Old Silk Road – was an extremely arduous trek for the intrepid and foolhardy, bearing little promise of reward and leading to little migration and intermingling of the races beyond the few Jews and Arabs, the Semitic races, who found livelihoods and remain in tiny pockets in the New World of the East.

The Chinese thus enjoy the greatest homogeneity of custom, language and culture of all the major races. They have also achieved the most uniformity in education and practice among the major tribes that make up their population: *Han, Man, Mong, Hui and*

Dzang. The Han are the dominant, core ethnic strand; the Manchus, descendants of the invading dynasty from Manchuria; the Mongols, descendants of invaders from North Central Asia; the Hui or Muslims in Xinjiang (formerly Chinese Turkestan); and the Dzang or Buddhist Tibetans.

If Darwin is to be believed, it might partly explain why the mythical Sun Wukong, the character Monkey in the classic story *Journey to the West*, enjoys such an exalted place in the pantheon of Chinese immortals. He is superbly wise, equal to anything and constantly evoked by the Chinese in a tacit nod to our supposedly common simian ancestry most recently observed in fossil discoveries. If indeed life is primarily about surviving and reproducing, then who are the Chinese to meddle with creation? (Or perhaps they could claim intelligent design for their one-child policy?) What we can intuit as we become increasingly acquainted with our fellow creatures from distant parts of the earth is a spontaneous empathy from those who make the effort to husband their resources, and use natural materials and energy sources for their sustenance. This is the distinctly human faculty for being peaceable, of drawing and being drawn by choice and nature into what the great German poet, Johann Wolfgang von Goethe, called 'elective affinities'. These are the real ties that bind us as humans.

Growth – the great shibboleth

As a measure of advancement or betterment, 'growth' has been reduced to a statistic: the year-on-year rate of increase in national GDP. China has determined that a minimum increase of 8 per cent has become imperative to pull the country out of poverty, and to prevent mass unemployment and social unrest. In the coming years this rate of growth is highly improbable and unlikely to be sustainable without heavy environmental pollution, debt-financed consumption and exploitation of dwindling natural resources. Thus, a truer measure of advancement, betterment and growth must be the extent to which most people may benefit from educational opportunities and the provision of an adequate safety net of social support; this will energize them to judge and take the risks necessary to create and increase the value-added of their work to an economy.

China's growth 'floor' of 8 per cent will become a stick for its own back unless it is recognized that no real growth can be achieved if the necessary balance between people and nature is awry; that is, if the country's ecology and the people's psychology (and food security) are broadly out of kilter. The social contract between Party and people will be threatened with breakdown unless the clamorous demands at the time of writing for affordable housing, health care and education can be satisfied. The government's avowed intent in its *bao ba* (literally 'save eight') campaign is to foster enough domestic consumer and industrial market demand to make up for the falling exports to the USA and Europe, and thereby bolster an emerging middle class in its confidence in spending more of its disposable income on goods and services rather than hoarding it in savings.

The failure of China's current economic model arises directly from its two major deficits: first, the environmental degradation that is the inevitable result of its industrial and manufacturing policies; and, second, the social tensions caused by the *bujun* (inequality of income) between urban and rural workers, the *hukou* (household registration) system, and the damage done to livelihoods by the abuse of land-use rights, and to literacy and health by inadequate provision of schools and hospitals.

Thus, the balance must be struck between GDP growth as the only measures of advancement and of local officials' performance and public welfare for the poor – whose basic subsistence is by no means assured. The government acknowledged this in early 2009 by giving one-off handouts to the poorest farmers to help them through the crisis. It has also allocated an extra US$120 billion over the next three years to upgrade health care facilities. Contraction in the economy caused jobs to dry up and millions of workers to be shed. Keeping these people and a further 6 million new graduates occupied in gainful employment will be the most pressing priority of the year. Unlike the West, the Chinese government is in a position to direct banks to grant loans to graduates to start new businesses (possibly on the scale of micro-finance) and to make allowances available to companies that employ them. In some cases, armed police have forced factory owners to pay workers. So it is now not power, but 'growth' that comes out of the barrel of a gun.

CHAPTER 14

Mastery

Consummate skill, knowledge and practice in a craft.
(A general Chinese understanding of Mastery)

Introduction

The stance of the Chinese military, though combat-ready at all times, is primarily defensive. Since the Russians are no longer considered a threat, there are no heavily manned garrisons along their frontiers; rather, the PLA is chiefly deployed to maintain internal security, particularly in the troublesome borderlands of Tibet and Xinjiang, where dissent and insurgency are most rife. The air force is well-equipped with jet fighters, bomber squadrons and long-range rockets and missiles, but it is the navy that plays the most crucial role in defending China's territory and disputed claims to islands and oil fields in the Yellow and South China Seas.

As the quality of life improves in China, the government is most concerned about maintaining not just territorial integrity, but also vital Chinese interests at home and abroad. Closest to home, of course, are the Taiwan Straits and the prospect of an eventual peaceful integration of Taiwan into the Motherland under a Special Administrative Region status, similar to but more complex and comprehensive than that accorded to Hong Kong. Abroad, there are vital shipping lanes to be guarded, not just the Straits of Malacca in South-East Asia, but also all those in the Western hemisphere used for international trade and transport of key oil and mineral supplies for China's growth and development. China has already sent a convoy of ships to police international waters off Somalia to help prevent piracy on the high seas. There is also its burgeoning sphere of influence in Latin America to be protected. All these are potential areas of conflict.

The budget for military spending is estimated to approach US$200 billion (around 4.5 per cent of GDP). China is now beginning to punch its weight and even above it, both politically and militarily. It is equipping its armed services with advanced weapons systems, nuclear submarines and long-range ballistic missiles for sustained operations at great distances. Its first aircraft carriers are now going into development and production. Sophisticated command and control computerization systems are now in place, and all the tools for covert cyber warfare have been devised to penetrate and embed themselves in Western defense systems. Since further nuclear non-proliferation treaties have been rendered effectively redundant by the wide availability and ease of assembly of nuclear materials and devices, there remain few ultimate deterrents beyond the threat of self-immolation and destruction by suicide bombers.

This puts the threat posed by North Korea, currently being defused by China, into a more tolerable perspective. The great dread of nuclear annihilation, which hung like a pall over the 1950s and 1960s, has in some way been diluted and dispelled. North Korea is, we believe, negotiating a family dynastic succession using nuclear warheads as bargaining chips. If you want to get noticed on the West, wield a big stick – a simple Asian imitation involves a radioactive one. The calm rationalism of a Chinese approach may yet play a part in banging Arab and Israeli, and Iranian and American, heads together, by persuading them that peaceful coexistence and mutual support is the only way to manage the struggle for survival on the planet.

From the back foot to the giant leap

China's sights are thus set on higher things. Its primary motivation in launching its space program is not to secure some kind of pre-emptive military or defensive strike but to restore the power balance with the West after two centuries of national humiliation at the hands of foreign interlopers. The West had stolen such a march on China in technical innovation by the nineteenth century that the country hardly dared to hope that it would ever recover the ground lost and the pattern of its glorious past. British naval power proved to be far superior to anything China could offer in resistance in the first, walkover war over opium in the 1830s. By the second opium war in 1860, European armies engaged in systematic routing. In the following account of the mindless destruction of the Old Summer Palace in Beijing, a 27-year-old captain in the Royal Engineers, Charles George Gordon, is presciently self-aware:

> We went out, and, after pillaging it, burned the whole place, destroying in a vandal-like manner most valuable property which [could] not be replaced for four millions. We got upward of £48 apiece prize money ... I have done well. The [local] people are very civil, but I think the grandees hate us, as they must after what we did to the palace. You can scarcely imagine the beauty and magnificence of the places we burnt. It made one's heart sore to burn them; in fact, these places were so large, and we were so pressed for time, that we could not plunder them carefully. Quantities of gold ornament were burnt, considered as brass. It was wretchedly demoralizing work for an army.

Machine-guns and rifle-fire were used to deadly effect against the Boxer Rebellion in 1900. Armed only with swords and staves, these bands of the Fists of the Righteous Harmony Society were trained *kung fu* fighters who claimed their supernatural powers would enable them to withstand being shot through in their devotion to the dowager empress.

After the Boxer Rebellion was crushed, China was fined war reparations of £67.5 million – equivalent to about US$6.6 billion today – for its temerity in offering resistance, and for the modest losses it caused to the eight foreign armies that had invaded its territory. Mercifully, a small portion of this money was redeemed through funding of the education of Chinese students in the USA. Perhaps Somalian piracy can be handled in Chinese fashion? Crush the pirates, demand reparations, then return the money as educational and medical aid.

The British and French looters and trashers of the Summer Palace in Beijing in 1860 have finally had their comeuppance: in a singular and dignified gesture of defiance in Paris, China bid but refused to pay for the bronze heads of a rat and a rabbit, representing Chinese birth signs, taken from the rim of a fountain at the Palace and which had found their way into the estate of the late Yves Saint Laurent in France. These items were carried off by troops under the command of Lord Elgin, son of the 'Elgin Marbles' Lord Elgin who scoured the Parthenon in Athens to furnish the British Museum. Shortly after this event came an unenforceable injunction from India to stop the sale at auction of Mahatma Gandhi's wire-rimmed spectacles, pocket watch and sandals at that time in the hands of a US film-maker. Small restitutions of these items will be far more than merely symbolic. They will amount to large and lasting redemptions for both sides. Purloined goods are, after all, still purloined goods.

Drawing down the moon

With its first manned spacewalk in 2008, China bounded back with a vengeance towards technical mastery and centre stage. Indeed, to demonstrate goodwill and to pre-empt space warfare, China even proposed a de-militarization of space, rejected out of hand by the USA, but China's main objective was accomplished: to restore national pride to its people and to burnish China's image in the international community. The power dividend from such an endeavor is incalculable in Chinese eyes. China does not seek to carve out control of its own 'space' and mastery of the skies and heavens as a final frontier; rather, it seeks to regain lost leadership and the initiative in exploration and the cutting edge in science and discovery that it enjoyed three centuries ago. It wishes to speak, act and be acknowledged as an equal in the international quest for progress and advancement in the human condition.

An unmanned lunar orbiter was launched in 2007. A permanent space station will be built, and a manned moon landing and exploration is planned for 2024. In 2006, China began its deep space exploration programme and plans an unmanned mission after 2014 and a manned phase after 2040. The desire to catch up with the Americans and the Russians knows no bounds. The chief designer of the Shenzhou spacecraft, Dr Qi Faren of the Chinese Academy of Sciences, said in a 2006 interview: 'Carrying out space programs is not just aimed at sending humanity into space *per se*, but instead at enabling humans to work in space normally, also preparing for the future manned exploration of Mars and Saturn.'

CHAPTER 15

Second Sight

The move from self-regulating capitalism to financial socialism is only a step.
(Attributed to Russian President Dimitry Medvedev)

Introduction

Globalization is an ever-increasing interdependence between countries in their trading and financial operations and systems. It has also meant for some time now – as swiftly became apparent in the autumn of 2008 – that the national banking authorities of individual countries have lost their ability to control and contain the effects of failure and fallout in financial globalization. National bank bailouts simply cannot cover the full scale of capital losses incurred from profligate lending; nor can they put effective limits on future contingent liabilities for taxpayers. The IMF and World Bank and the European Bank for Reconstruction and Development are not designed to deal with this eventuality, nor do they yet have the capacity to do so. There has thus been a chronic disjunction in the provision of credit as the lifeblood of businesses, since the very capital ratios and reserve requirements that enabled banks to lend prudently have been swept away by the avalanche of bad debt.

Apportioning blame for our dire predicament at this point is largely futile. It is more instructive to examine the main contributory causes to the breakdown of sound money and the loss of confidence in the global financial system. It may then be possible to perceive the outline of the kind of supranational institution that will need to be configured to ensure the conservation of underlying value in loan transactions of the future. We can begin with the ballooning imbalances in trade occasioned by China's massive export drive to supply the USA with cheap manufactured goods and services.

This caused a corresponding pile-up of Chinese reserves in US dollars, invested mainly in US Treasury Bills, which glut led indirectly to fuelling the reckless mortgage lending by US and international banks. To work their assets harder – which had become the first injunction of all bankers – the banks resorted to repackaging their debt as derivative products and selling them on in a process of obfuscation, syndication and dilution by the financial engineers, as if they could in that way lay off the risks inherent in the low underlying value of these products. The Americans may point their finger at the Chinese, accusing them of 'manipulating the currency' or keeping it artificially low to suppress natural appreciation and price rises for their exports – thereby obtaining an 'unfair' competitive advantage. The Chinese, for their part, may point to unbridled Western over-consumption and irresponsible lending and regulatory practices as precipitating the downfall of the West's systems of financial liberalization.

What each side fails sufficiently to take into account is the sea change in international capital flows that has occurred since Bretton Woods and the IMF were set up to facilitate and regulate them in 1944. These institutions were designed primarily for state-to-state transactions, while the majority of current international capital flows are private transactions – including a maelstrom of fools' gold sucked in on a promise of unwavering returns by Bernard Madoff (in pyramid schemes) and Allen Stanford (in Caribbean banking) from institutional and private investors worldwide. A system and mechanisms for checks and balances to regulate this traffic is now urgently needed if the free flow of trade- and peace-enhancing funds is to be resumed.

Almost by default, China has become the world's banker, since it now has the lion's share of global savings. While it acknowledges its umbilical ties to the USA as a source of most of these savings, it is in no way predisposed to take any initiative toward restoring a workable global financial system, unless its place and interests in the new order are fully accounted for in the architecture of its new trading and financial systems. Such systems, and such an institutional framework, must be devised in short order among the leading locomotive members of the G20 before the world descends into financial anarchy and the protectionism of predatory and competing nationalisms.

This new order will have to learn to live with a much reduced private sector, while new investment will be dictated increasingly by state capitalism, given the rapid pace of nationalization of so many of the world's proudly independent financial institutions. The Chinese government can order banks to lend. They can also direct and specify to which industries and companies loans should be granted, and thus orchestrate and protect the development of favoured industrial sectors. These industries are likely to be those dedicated to the proliferation of innovation in new product conception and design, environmental protection and information technology.

To achieve its goals in these areas, China needs outside knowledge and assistance. It may have the money but it does not have all the means. If it can obtain assurances of inclusion as a ranking member, by investing a fraction of its reserves, in any successor organization to the IMF or World Bank – which must perforce have much greater international authority – then its rise may yet be peaceful and the impact of its policies beneficial and benign. As some humorous Confucians have already suggested, not entirely in jest, the chronology of China's recent development could soon read:

1949   Socialism saves China

1979   Capitalism saves China

1989   China saves socialism

2009   China saves capitalism

2019   China saves the planet.

Values

The financial tsunami of late 2008 exposed the raw vulnerabilities of the West and threw them into sharp relief. For the more ruthless and brutal command-and-control regimes of Russia, North Korea, Burma and Sudan there is reversion to Cold War tensions. Western values of democracy, human rights, environmental protection, control of the proliferation of weapons of mass destruction, free trade, the rule of law, freedom of the press and religion have little or no place on their agenda. The ideal of a 'Western-centered, open, integrated, rule-based, international order' suddenly appears to be naïve in the extreme in the face of the cold stare of such 'Godless dictatorships'. China is not such a one. It seeks to assume its rightful place in the world and on its own terms. It reaches out to the world, when others turn inwards. It expects the West to acknowledge its stature as a major power and to accord it the status to which it feels entitled as a key player and partner in international trade and investment. This means a permanent seat at the tables of the world's councils, with full voting rights appropriate to its geopolitical, military and economic standing.

This process has already begun, with the first G20 meeting, held in London in early 2009, bringing the Chinese into global discussion on economic affairs. But perhaps the most telling acknowledgement of China's true place in the modern world was led by the Western military. The only Secretary General of NATO to invoke Article 5 (an 'attack one, attack all' type of clause), Lord Robertson of Port Ellen, pointed out in a recent speech celebrating sixty years of NATO, that he had personally contacted the Chinese government to advise them of the NATO deployment to Afghanistan. The Chinese, he said, were most concerned over stability in the region and would be pleased if NATO forces could maintain this and quell any uprising.

In *China Calling*, we argue that China's actions can be understood if their basic principle of stability at any cost is used to interpret those actions. China's current granite face and stance is apparently inimical to the recognition of human rights, heedless of nuclear proliferation, careless of environmental degradation, and intolerant of troublesome border peoples and neighboring countries from Tibet to Taiwan. Within China's walled world, however, there is a quiet agitation for reform of the country's political system. Outright democracy is not envisaged; but some restriction on the power of the Party is, since the backwardness and unwieldiness of the current system and chain of command is affecting the even pace of economic development and is seen as a brake on real social development. For the sake of Party stability, the rights of ordinary people, the press, lawyers, Buddhists and Christians are all to be extended to ease the inclusion of all citizens in the 'democratic' process of participation in law- and decision-making.

The Party will, of course, still maintain its elitist overall control of this process. This means that the Chinese will continue to stonewall when pressed for definitions of either socialism or democracy. This is because Deng Xiaoping's 'Reform and Opening' pulled off the singular feat of a transformation of the economy under the blanket banner 'Socialism with Chinese characteristics'. When the meaning of socialism is queried, the answer is invariably, 'The continuing rule of the Chinese Communist Party'. As for democracy, the explanation is much more straightforward. Democracy is to be developed over time, but over a period long enough to enfranchise a gradually growing middle class with sufficient education and understanding of the world to exercise it. This seems to have much in common with the old Western restriction of the vote to those who owned property. China is now allowing private property purchases, but the democratic process appears to be towards an electorate based on intellectual property – only those with meritocracy in mind can wield a ballot paper. In the West, 18-year-old junkies on benefit (and bankers subsidized by taxes) can exercise the same voting power as professionals, servicemen and women, and hardworking taxpayers. China will not let that style of universal suffrage happen. After all, the purpose of democracy is to let those who understand it, then use it as a form of self-governance – for the people, by the people. Letting those who do not understand it, or are unable to use it, is not a Chinese objective.

It would be a grave misconception, however, to assume that China will lapse into pure nationalism; the reverse is more likely. The last thing that China needs or wants is to be seen as defensive and inward-looking, like the 'us-against-the-world' autocracies. For its own sustenance and maintenance it depends on foreigners' goodwill and cooperation more than ever before and fully realizes this. Securing vital oil and mineral resources from Africa, Australia and Latin America will entail extensive 'public diplomacy' and engagement with foreign governments at both commercial and cultural levels. Overseas investment, stock exchange listings and the expansion of markets for their branded goods all depend on the Chinese being perceived as attractive and trustworthy partners. If state-owned enterprises are to be the main chosen instruments for the advance of state capitalism on the world stage, then let this be acknowledged as a purely pragmatic move toward the effective transformation and integration of China's economy into the global system. This is hardly incompatible with an eventual rule of law and the norms of corporate and acknowledged forms of democratic governance.

Cross-reach

Once we examine the writings of cosmopolitan philosophers, poets and playwrights, it rapidly appears that Chinese culture and the Chinese psyche are nothing like as remote, impenetrable or obscure as we might at first have believed. In fact, the influence of Chinese original thought, arts and aesthetics is plain to see if we care to look at the way it has impressed itself on the Western mind. From the somewhat romantic and fanciful notions of China entertained from close at hand by Marco Polo and the Jesuit, Matteo Ricci, and from afar by Oliver Goldsmith and Voltaire, it has long had a captivating effect. Later authors have tended to perpetuate rather than to diminish the power of myth and the mystic East. Gottfried Leibniz and Leo Tolstoy were great champions of Chinese philosophy in the nineteenth century, while Carl Jung, Bertolt Brecht and Ezra Pound carried the torch for China in the twentieth century. Arthur Waley's translation of classical Chinese poetry opened up a delightful new window on the world, while Somerset Maugham caught the spirit of colonial days and Sax Rohmer stirred needless antipathy with his confabulation, the fiendish Dr Fu Manchu.

From the Chinese perspective came the friendly interpolations from East to West of Lin Yutang and Chiang Yee, while Ernest Bramah, with his Kai Lung stories, and Robert van Gulik and his Judge Dee detective tales did much to familiarize Western readers with Chinese powers of observation and deduction. Today, there are numerous accounts of the *Wild Swans* genre available to explain the harsh realities of the Cultural Revolution and to document in oral histories, such as Xinran's *China Witness*, the extraordinary arcs of the lives of ordinary people over the twentieth century. Films such as *The Blue Kite*, Bernardo Bertolucci's *The Last Emperor* and Chen Kaige's epic *Farewell, My Concubine* have brought China graphically alive to Western audiences. Chinese painting, calligraphy and *tai chi* have all entered the mainstream of the world's pleasures and pastimes. The first Chinese person to win the Nobel Prize for

Literature was Gao Xingjian in 2000. This was awarded for 'an oeuvre of universal validity, bitter insights and linguistic ingenuity, which has opened new paths for the Chinese novel' – albeit honed through the prism of a wider world view via exile in France.

Education and distance learning

Try as they might, the Party and the schooling system in China cannot quite dispel the notion that it is elitist in its selection procedures and in its perpetuation of self-selecting hierarchies in the administration of government and in the creation and management of business enterprises. In spite of serious efforts at social engineering and substantial scholarship funding for poor students to complete secondary and tertiary education, just over 10 per cent of Chinese students go through higher education. There are thus grave inequalities of opportunity and access between the urban middle classes and the rural poor. The limited teaching resources, the sheer numbers of students and the distances involved in reaching them all conspire to make this access extremely difficult.

This disparity is exacerbated by the special treatment and attention given to top students at elite universities, who are pressured into studying for up to sixteen hours a day every day of the week and then made subject to a cull of the lowest 10 per cent at the end of the academic year – the real meaning of decimation. Interestingly, Chinese graduate students in the UK claim to be more knowledgeable after long (four to five) years of such passive absorption of technical subjects, but readily concede that Western counterparts are rather more adept at articulating what they think and believe about the practical application of these subjects.

One way of bridging the gap in access between urban and rural students in China is via online teaching. The biggest bottleneck is, of course, access to computers and broadband services, and that e-learning tends to be transmitted to large classes of 300–400 students with minimal scope for interaction and discussion with teachers. The government is challenged with maintaining a tricky balancing act: providing the rural poor with an adequate access to education, so that they are not forced to move to the cities in search of it. In spite of the difficulty of providing formal, face-to-face, teacher-led courses to the mass of students, one positive development and new worldwide phenomenon may partially compensate for this: the access available via the web to academic papers, podcasts and videos from around the world, which is radically altering the way that learning is acquired.

In December 1978, when the USA recognized Beijing, the first fifty Communist Party Chinese students were sent abroad to study in the USA. By 2006, this figure had passed 1 million. Between 1847 and 1978, only 130,000 Chinese students had travelled overseas. Thus, the thirty years since 1978 have shown a tenfold increase in these numbers. As college entrance exams get harder, with up to 10 million students competing for places every year, many are seeking alternative places overseas. The majority of students go to the USA, Britain and Europe, but many more now go to Australia, Canada and South-East Asian countries. However, of these 1 million plus students (around 15 per cent of overseas students worldwide), less than a third have returned to China to live and work. This proportion is now rising steadily with the increased opportunities offered by China as it extends its operations both at home and overseas. Most popular subjects for students are the sciences, and international business management and finance, including the MBA program, which equip them for careers in innovation, R&D (research and development) and multinational management positions. These returnees are best placed to translate, interpret and bridge both Chinese and Western cultures.

China's new age

The step change in Chinese life and living standards since the late 1970s, and the start of the Reform and Opening movement has meant that many of the quaint, old-fashioned notions and tenets of traditional morality in China – trust, loyalty, filial piety, even ancestor worship – have seemingly been swept aside. The onrush of a market economy and the unremitting progress of development have left most Chinese families fixated on the acquisition of material goods and the worship of money. While the market economy has brought great benefit and a growing sense of self-reliance to the people, it has been adopted with scant concern for the framing of ethical codes and practices in its operation.

Thus, malpractice is rife – from petty corruption (paid advocacy) and embezzlement at the provincial government level, to rampant counterfeiting and faking of industrial and consumer branded goods with no heed being paid and very little enforcement of patent law or intellectual property rights protection. There is much hand-wringing over the lack of any ethical guidelines on standards of minimally acceptable conduct and practice in business. There has also been a widespread collapse of what the Chinese call 'virtue', or what in the West might be called 'integrity'. The damning phrase, *quede*, meaning 'lacking in virtue', has now lost all its force as an indictment of dishonest conduct and no longer has the power to stigmatize wrongdoers or label them as rogues or pariahs. A devilish drive of 'needs must' prevails over a civil sense of decency, probity and honor. Most of this is a result of disillusionment at life under fifty years of a communist doctrinaire regime, followed by the corroding effects of a pragmatic but undignified capitalism.

At the base of this spiritual and existential malaise is the loss of a coherent national ideology with a political system to match it. The Cultural Revolution caused communism in China to self-destruct, leaving the mass of the people with no ethical compass, no magnetic pole in the moral maze, with all other traditional beliefs thoroughly discredited and outlawed. Outright religious beliefs were derided and proscribed as being backward and anathema by an avowedly atheist communist government. Traditional Taoist, Buddhist and Christian ceremonies and services were driven underground, and Confucius himself was relegated to the status of a malign influence, which could only hold the Chinese people back from fulfilling their destiny. The reversion since the 1980s to a more ordered and stratified society of rich and poor has seen the rise of a new class of unscrupulous officials, who have learned to exploit small businesses in particular, extorting bribes and beggaring their operations, generally with impunity.

What, then, is to fill this void in values and beliefs to live by? While Confucianism seems to be enjoying a gradual resurgence and even a reinstatement at an official level (witness the establishment of the talismanic 'Confucius Institutes' worldwide), this is only a possible ideological solution to the challenge of cultural continuity and the grand narrative of Chinese self-esteem and standing in the world. Will this in itself be sufficient to bring about a restoration of moral standards in public and private life – if it is taught rigorously as a system of ethics in schools? It has, after all, been the backbone and moral fibre of Chinese identity and character over two millennia.

After years of being expected to present a shining and compliant public face under Mao, the Chinese citizen is now at last allowed to retreat into a private world of his or her own and a contemplation or recitation of the Buddhist sutras or, more popularly, the *Tao Te Ching*, the great scriptural canon of Lao-tzu, Old Master to Confucius. To the Chinese, the *Tao* (literally, 'the Way') has much the same ineffable meaning as 'the Word' in St. John's Gospel in the Bible. The central tenet of the faith is the oneness of humankind with nature, and the acquiring of merit and virtue towards immortality through doing good deeds and helping others. To Lu Xun, the best known Chinese writer of the early twentieth century, the Chinese spirit was simply rooted in Taoism, which has a special place in Chinese culture as the one truly indigenous religion. Taoism hallowed the practice of medicine and chemistry, and its attempts at alchemy and the creation of elixirs led to the discovery of gunpowder. It shares with Christianity its close connection with medicine, based on maintaining the 'spirit level' of the *qi* or life force, largely through breathing exercises and a technique of using energy from within one body to draw out the *qi* from another. While Western medicine focuses on keeping the cells healthy and the red and white corpuscles in balance, this Eastern remedy focuses on the *qi* or vital energy as the most refined, albeit immaterial, component of the physical body.

Although it shares certain deep breathing techniques or *qi gong*, the Falun Gong movement is outlawed and persecuted as being deviant and evil in China, chiefly because its leader is perceived by the Party as a rival authority to the state (haunted by the memory of Hong Xinquan, the self-proclaimed younger brother of Jesus Christ, and his eleven-year reign over his Taiping Heavenly Kingdom of much of northern China from 1853 to 1864). Falun Gong is also deemed to pose a social threat to more feeble-minded people. who donate money to the movement they can ill afford and even forgo necessary medical treatment out of superstition.

After sixty years in power, the Party is becoming reconciled slowly to the strength of the Christian churches in China. Long suspected of being infiltrators, spies and subverters of minority peoples in the country, Christian missionaries have left a deep and lasting legacy. The Catholic Church has always been held at bay and tightly monitored, as the Vatican is still seen as a rival power in statehood and authority for Chinese hearts and minds. Protestant churches, however, abound throughout the country and have become a vital social force to be reckoned with, a phenomenon the Party has reluctantly recognized and acknowledged as not posing a threat to civil order or obedience. While officially sanctioned Church members number about 5 million Catholics and 21 million Protestants, the true numbers are probably over 100 million more, given the proliferation of 'house' churches, where gatherings of no more than twenty-five people may take place within the law on public assembly.

The Christian Church in China thus outnumbers the membership of the Communist Party in China (74 million) in the same way as the number of people learning English in China outnumbers the total of native English-speakers in the world. The Heng Shan Community Church in Shanghai is a medium-sized building, but the people keep coming in: for the 10 o'clock Sunday service there must be at least 500 in attendance, with another 100 watching and joining the service on closed circuit television in the annex outside. There are familiar hymns in Chinese and a bracing 20-minute sermon. Communion is certainly a logistical triumph: first wafers, then tiny cups of wine are passed along the pews, so that everyone takes and receives.

The missionary presence in China is no longer simply tolerated, still less reviled, but quietly supported and tacitly encouraged by the Party for the humanitarian and development assistance it provides in difficult areas populated by minority peoples. Although there is an absolute prohibition on proselytizing or propagating the Christian doctrine, the trend set by the ministry of organizations such as the Salvation Army, registered as non-government organizations, like Oxfam, in providing traditional primary health care (including AIDS prevention), adult literacy training and environmental protection assistance, is exemplary. It also serves as a model operation for the Chinese as they view the potential for their own outreach in Africa and Latin America. The extreme sensitivity that these initiatives aroused in the past, arising mainly from fear that they would lead to the subversion and separatism of minority peoples through missions' covert support of local independence movements, has been largely dispelled.

The future of China may thus be determined in part by a marriage of convenience between Confucian rectitude, ritual and tradition, and the liberating power of modern Christianity to give fresh meaning and context to the demands of business and 'scientific development'. Indeed, such a marriage may leave the more atheistic elements of liberal democracy and *laissez-faire* capitalism well behind.

Obamarama

In his speech marking the occasion of the thirtieth anniversary of Reform and Opening, President Hu Jintao urged the PLA 'to strengthen its ability to engage in non war-related operations'; that is, to act as local militia to quell riots and defuse anti-government demonstrations. In this way, many cracks in the social compact may be papered over temporarily, but the bargain struck between Party and people, whereby jobs are secured at the cost of a cession of political control, must at all events be kept, if the Party is to prevail. He then lapsed into opaque, 'agit-prop' parlance, urging the people to further respect the 'organic synthesis' of the Party's goals: 'upholding Party leadership; letting the people be masters of the country; and running the country according to law'. No matter that both he and Premier Wen Jiabao also took to the moral high ground in laying the blame for the global crisis squarely at the West's door, economic realities have tended to render such rhetoric hollow and redundant. This global crisis has damaged the economic synergy between China and the USA. China's export/investment economic model and the US consumer credit/capital model have both reached the end of their useful working lives.

The odd period of disjunction and hiatus in early 2009 following the inauguration of President Barack Obama in the USA served to heighten tensions between China as an emerging power in the world and the USA as the established prevailing influence. China envies the USA its leadership in world affairs. It publicly questioned the US sense of 'a divinely granted destiny, no matter what other nations may think'. It fears the spread of democratic values and worries about the encircling alliances of democracy in Asia – from Japan to the ASEAN countries. But it also sees US authority weakened by two unwise 'wars on terror' and its attention distracted from Asia, where China has made vast inroads by promoting itself as the only real 'Asian' power.

It perceives all too well how much better Obama understands than Bush did the uses and potential of American power and influence – and above all, the power of example, of the sheer charisma of leadership that follows in the footsteps of Franklin D. Roosevelt, John F. Kennedy and Ronald Reagan – a factor plainly missing in Chinese political life since the days of Mao, Chou and Deng, and possibly Zhao Ziyang. Obama spoke directly in his inaugural address about facing down fascism and communism, and how those who silence dissent are on 'the wrong side of history'. Formerly, this would have meant Russia; this time it meant China. The gauntlet has thus been thrown down in the war of competing visions and attractions.

That gauntlet does not at present contain a particularly steely fist. Failure of the US capital finance system and the precipitous fall in demand for Chinese goods has forced China to domesticate its economic growth model and reduce its dependence on the US economic system. This 'bridging loan' of US demand for its exports is still urgently required to keep its workers in employment until China can become self-sufficient. The *quid pro quo* is Chinese finance for US debt to help fund the US$800 billion bailout. Collaboration is a cultural and economic expedient. Much more seriously contentious is the issue of climate change, which is set to tax severely the capacity of each side to work together. China is the world's leading emitter of CO_2, but per capita emissions in the USA remain four times greater than China's. This is by far the greatest political challenge in the China–West relationship, and one that requires not just 'engagement', but some 'down-and-dirty' teamwork in emissions recording, low-cost green and coal technology, and energy efficiency and conservation. This is the kind of challenge that cannot be evaded, a facing up to dealing jointly with a common scourge to health and human progress. Is this not what Confucius meant by 'harmony', and Christ meant by 'love thy neighbor as thyself'? East and West have much in common but are often commonly misunderstood.

Points to ponder

Points

Depending how you count creditors and debtors or GDP or wealth per head of population, China has overtaken Germany as the third-largest economic power in the world and is heading for the top. Chinese power is the one that counts – the West has had its chance but lost its financial head. The West's loss may, however, be the world's gain.

China is under pressure for supporting dodgy African regimes, for oppression in Tibet, for opposing democratic freedom for Taiwan, for suppressing Xinjiang autonomy, for aiding military succession planning in Burma, and for non-involvement in the 'internal affairs' of those nations it wishes to maintain in power. But then the USA and UK have had very similar charges laid against them – in the Philippines, in Vietnam, in South Africa, in Egypt, in Israel, in Iraq, in Somalia, in Honduras, in Afghanistan, in countries that suit their domestic needs.

China will therefore continue its global diplomatic protection, financial aid and military support to countries and nations whose survival will help China maintain and defend its borders and supply lines. China ensures that its understanding of the games played in the global arena is expanded. The largest number of delegates to all United Nations missions is provided by China. China has been represented on the UN Security Council since it was formed after the Second World War. China has its own satellites, aircraft and nuclear industries, defence industry, manufacturing bases, education and engineering industries – and cash to boot. As the old saying goes, 'He who pays the piper calls the tune', and with China a 'little worried' about where its cash reserves may now reside, the piper at the new dawn will be playing a Chinese flute.

The world will gain, therefore, by playing alongside China. There is no need for sycophantic dancing to China's tune, but there is a need for reciprocal harmonies. Much of China's difficulties with the West have been through a mutual misunderstanding of policy – domestic, foreign and military. The need for transparency in actions at home and abroad applies to Western powers as well as to China. The threat of protectionism in international economic affairs, a rise in trade barriers, creates instability in domestic security. The mandate of the Chinese Communist Party is dependent on home security and a continuing confidence in the future development of the nation. This confidence can be increased by the involvement of China in all world matters – not just financial, not just political, but a redevelopment of the UN to allow equality for the so called developing nations, and defined by Westerners to include the nation of China.

Ponder

There is still fear that China's control over the world economy, especially over its credit to the USA, will be used to damage the West. Not so – the West has demonstrated that it is quite capable of financially damaging itself. The leading indicator for global instability is the expansion of China's deep water navy. China knows that policing of piracy off the Gulf of Aden is excellent acceptable international practice for the protection of its own cargo routes – through the Straits of Malacca, Straits of Taiwan and channels into the East China Sea and the Yellow Sea off the Korean peninsula. With the global economy diverting Chinese stimulus packages into infrastructure and defence rather than into manufacturing, the aircraft carriers of the Chinese navy – perhaps due for trials in 2012 – will herald a new world order.

If we had to sum up the main message of this book, it is to acknowledge the need for reciprocity in dealings with China. Do not use ill-defined and poorly structured economic arguments to attack the country. Do 'misunderestimate' (to use former President George W. Bush's double negative) its strength and desire to secure its borders. Do not overestimate its ability and desire to take the lead in the world. China wishes to work together with the West, not confront it. If the West fails to understand how to treat China, then the league table of global power will show a continuing loss for liberal democracy and a gain for centralized imperialism. China, a nation with millennia of experience in running itself, is rightfully counting down to a seat at the round table of global rule.

Postscript

Protectionism is now a major issue for national governments. Protection is sought from competing ideologies – religious, economic, political and cultural. Open capitalism and financial power are entertained in the West, facing a Confucian social challenge from the East. Obstinate, stubborn sanctions are mistakenly used as defenses against military and trading advances from North and South Asia and from China. Conflicting national interests lead to confrontation in global goals.

Money has been an artificial but decisive control in the analysis of growth. Economists assume that nations are developed or undeveloped dependent upon the income *per capita*. This manifest error has led to Western excess and the present and previous recessions. Food stability and energy security are true measures of growth, the former allowing survival and the latter creating freedom. Both must be encouraged in China as in the West. Although our postscript is written before the Copenhagen meeting on global warming, being more of a prescript, the human reality is that survival and freedom now need social collaboration not competitive capitalism.

References

Our references are sectioned by Part number and by Chapter number/section. Where we have taken ideas or concepts from other authors for argument or discussion, then their book, journal or newspaper article is referenced. Where direct quotations are used, these are specified against page number of book, journal etc. Where we have read interesting articles which gave us food for thought, we have put them into the general reference list as they may prove interesting to others. Where we have written from our own experience or from anecdotes heard over the years, we have either preserved the anonymity of our sources or have written from memories of the events themselves. For business and management practitioners, the intelligence and experience gathered from lengthy discussion into the night are often remembered not for their intensity, but for their consequences. We are publishing the more useful results.

Part I – Politics, opportunism, environment, might, society

In the introduction to Part I, we have taken our starting point as our 2008 book *China Calling: A Foot in the Global Door*. Much of what we said in that book remains correct today, and we have felt no major need to alter our previous stance. *China Calling* provides a constancy of insights which help explain variation in events today. It abounds with references – both particular and general – and can be read in conjunction with Part I. We have, however, updated our information from sources shown below.

Chapter 1: Introduction

Orwell's comment on eccentricity comes from *Burmese Days*. The quote from Francis Fukuyama on Chinese culture and economic practices can be found in his book *Trust – The Social Virtues and the Creation of Prosperity.*

Chapter 1: Politics

The African comment on nylon strings was overheard in Beijing but seems appropriate. Information on the party Congress of 2009 comes from *Xinhua* news agency but is reinterpreted after discussion with our respondents in China. Source of the data shown in Table I.1 is the published position of the US Department of Treasury and Federal Reserve. It can be accessed on: www.treas.gov/tic/mfh.txt.

Chapter 2: Opportunism

The research by Haley and Tan (1999) can be found in the general references. Our comments on the Royal Bank of Scotland were interpreted from various sources: primarily from professional sources in Edinburgh, Scotland. Basic geographical knowledge and the references in our first book help interpret this chapter.

Chapter 3: Environment

The ideas of 'bounded rationality' and 'satisficing' are by Herbert Simon. Our observations during visits to China and discussions with respondents have highlighted many of the environmental problems facing China. The *China Daily* reports on a regular basis on major problems, but much information is retained by Chinese officials.

Chapter 4: Might

Our interpretation of Taiwan's position *vis-à-vis* China is based on many years of living there. The activities of the PLA during the Szechuan earthquake were reported on Chinese television, in the national press and by news agencies worldwide, as is much of the general information on China's activities. It is the interpretation of those activities that generally needs critical thinking.

Chapter 5: Society

Reports on the Party Congress are from *Xinhua* news agency and reinterpreted following our discussions with respondents in China. The *Analects* of Confucius are available from many sources but the reader may enjoy the summary by Walter Slote and George de Vos called 'Confucianism and the Family'.

Part II – Power, opportunities, equilibrium, military, science

The introduction to Part II notes that China's reaction to Western commentary has been notoriously prickly and defensive. Now, with its new-found financial strength and confidence, its tone has become much more assertive and self-assured. We also refer to an interview with Gao Xijing by James Fallows – 'Be nice to the countries that lend you money', *The Atlantic*, December 2008. Different views on human rights are explained by Zhao Qizheng, director-general of the State Council Information Office, in an article in the *People's Daily*, February 11, 2002. 'The Chinese Model of Development' is explained by Dr Wei Pan, a professor at the School of International Studies, Peking University, in a paper presented in London, October 11, 2007. Our findings are based on our own research and an in-depth survey carried out by Professor Greg Philo of Glasgow University Media Group – *The Impact of Direct Experience on Evaluation of British and Chinese Societies* (2008). The readings recommended are a random selection designed to broaden the mind and the view of the world from different perspectives.

Chapter 6: Power

Changes in power shifts are regularly documented from a Chinese perspective by *Xinhua* news agency but are interpreted through our discussions in China.

Chapter 7: Opportunities

Public diplomacy is used in the sense of launching a new brand or image of China rising rather than in any propagandist sense. We describe the closely guarded world of Chinese immigrants, in which a conspiracy of silence is based on a common feeling that illegal immigration is a fact of life : 'We had hard times when we came over, so why should we help?' ... 'Hardship is a way of sorting the lazy from the strong, the ones who work hard will get rich eventually.' 'D' notices are official requests from the UK Ministry of Defence to news editors not to publish or broadcast certain items for reasons of national security. Source of data: Council on Foreign Relations; World Bank; Worldfocus. Latin America source of data: The Jamestown Foundation; *Wall Street Journal*, November 20, 2008.

Chapter 8: Equilibrium

Source of data: The US Department of Energy/Energy Information Administration; National Energy Bureau (China); *China Daily*; 'Energy Blue Paper' (Chinese Academy of Social Sciences).

Chapter 9: Military

There are many who comment on China, but much of the information here came from our own discussions with respondents in China and Taiwan.

Chapter 10: Science

Our primary sources for discussion relate to documents from the International Monetary Fund (IMF); Organisation for Economic Co-operation and Development (OECD); World Health Organization (WHO); George Orwell's parody of I Corinthians is from *Keep the Aspidistra Flying*; and the loss of 'domain knowledge' is addressed in Kenneth Hopper and William Hopper, *The Puritan Gift: Triumph, Collapse and Revival of an American Dream* (I. B. Tauris, 2007).

Part III – Potential, outcomes, evolution, mastery, second sight

This part is more predictive and is designed to challenge as well as report.

Chapter 11: Potential

An excellent source is Michael Collins, in his paper, 'China's Confucius and Western Democracy', *Contemporary Review*, vol. 296, no. 1689, Summer 2008, which provides a lucid analysis. Further issues were also addressed in *'The Elephant and the Dragon'*, a paper presented at the Alumni Weekend at the Said Business School, Oxford, by Dr Rajiv Lall, CEO of the Infrastructure Development Finance Company Ltd (IDFC, Mumbai) on September 20, 2008.

Chapter 12: Outcomes

Source of data: J. P. Morgan Investment Management.

Chapter 13: Evolution

We are also prompted by the *Earth Enterprise* report, first published by Interplan Research and J M Pick in 1973; and an article in *The Times* of November 17, 2008, 'The energy miser leaving tiny carbon footprint in her wake'.

Sources of data: Climate Change Group (UK); National Energy Bureau (China).

Chapter 14: Mastery

The Charles George Gordon account is from www.pekinheaven. com/history1.htm.

Sources of data: Royal United Services Institute (RUSI).

Chapter 15: Second sight

Our interpretation of respondents' comments is framed by 'The Making of a Mess – Who Broke Global Finance, and Who Should Pay for It', Harold James, *Foreign Affairs*, January/February 2009. On education, regular articles in the press provide background information, particularly *The Guardian*, January 20, 2009.

Glossary and Index

We have not put in place a keyword index as we have used executive style summaries at the beginning of each part of the book. We believe that this is preferable for the modern reader. From an academic perspective, the structure of the book is holistic, with the word *guanxi* constantly cross-referencing with other concepts, thus making any index overly long and very complicated.

We do, however, present a brief introduction to Chinese pronunciation and several important and useful concepts in this glossary. The glossary provides a brief explanation of concepts discussed in the text and indexes where they are first used.

To aid the reader, we should explain that Chinese pronunciation is linked to the Roman spelling more directly than English (think about the difference in pronunciation between cough and bough). Thus *ch* is as in 'cheese', *q* is as in 'job' and *x* is as in 'she'. *Qingdao* is thus pronounced 'Jingdow'.

The vowels form the tongue and mouth movements (*xiao* equals shyaow). Vowels are more French-sounding than English (*u* is ooh rather than you). Tones are very important — *mai* with rising and then falling vowels means to buy, *mai* with a distinct falling tone is to sell. We do not go into detail but merely warn the reader to be careful lest the transaction goes the wrong way.

Term	Meaning	Page
ba bao	literally 'save eight', ensure an 8 per cent growth rate.	154
balinghou	the generation born after 1980.	140
Boxer Rebellion	the 1900 uprising by the 'Righteous Fists of Harmony' fighters against invading European armies.	189

Deng Xiaoping	Chinese Communist leader and prime mover of economic reform and opening up of relations with the West from the late 1970s.	30
fa	Rules, laws and strict principles.	142
Falun Gong	Chinese spiritual discipline, based on meditation and breathing exercises, outlawed by the CCP.	6
fa zhi	Rule by law, rather than rule of law (as opposed to *ren zhi*, rule by humankind).	85
feng shui	Chinese geomancy, the art of siting buildings auspiciously.	77
G20	Group of twenty finance ministers and central bank governors from Argentina, Australia, Brazil, Canada, China, France, Germany, India, Indonesia, Italy, Japan, Mexico, Russia, Saudi Arabia, South Africa, South Korea, Turkey, the UK, the USA and the EU. Main forum for cooperation and co-ordination of the global financial system.	133
guanxi	Literally 'relationship', but used to mean 'connections' or the network of relationships formed and used by Chinese individuals to achieve their ends, based on mutual obligation and common understanding.	4
Han Dynasty	The period of rule by the dominant (*Han*) ethnic group (206 BC to 220 AD), which later dynasties took as a model for the ordering of society.	75
hukou	Chinese household registration system, based on residency permits.	138

KMT	Kuomintang, the Chinese Nationalist Party, led by Chiang Kai-shek.	19
kowtow	The old Chinese ritual of touching the ground with the forehead in submission to the emperor and high officials.	3
Legalism	One of the four main Chinese schools of philosophy (the others are Confucianism, Taoism and Mohism). A pragmatic code, based on rewarding those who obey the law and punishing those who break it.	101
Legge	The Revd Dr James Legge, Scottish Sinologist, first Professor of Chinese at Oxford University (1876–97).	161
li	Ritual, the conduct of relationships.	85
Lin Yutang	Twentieth-century Chinese writer of popular works such as *My Country and My People*, who did much to explain and interpret the East to the West.	196
Lu Xun	Best-known Chinese writer of the early twentieth century, something of a Chinese Rudyard Kipling in his capture of the spirit of the times in the demotic language of the new Republic.	200
luan, da luan	Literally, 'great chaos', much feared if as a result of a breakdown of civil society.	20
Mao Zedong	Chinese communist leader and Chairman of the Chinese Communist Party from 1949 to 1976.	30

Marco Polo	Italian adventurer who travelled from Venice to China between 1271 and 1275, and was received by the court of Kublai Khan. His account of his travels awakened European interest in trade with the East.	196
Manchu	People originating in Manchuria, founders of the Qing Dynasty.	185
Meng Tzu	Mencius, the most influential philosopher and interpreter (around 300 BC) of Confucian ideas.	158
mianzi	Literally, 'face', but used to mean the individual's sense of self-image and worth, and the respect shown to others in both word and deed.	80
Ming Dynasty	Chinese dynasty from 1368 to 1644, overthrown by the Manchus (see Qing Dynasty).	56
Needham's Puzzle	Joseph Needham, author of *Science and Civilization in China*, was confounded by China's failure to develop into a major power in the nineteenth century, given that it had the world's largest economy in the eighteenth century.	70
Opium Wars	The first Opium War was fought between the British East India Company and the Qing Dynasty over access to opium trading from 1839 to 1842. The Second Opium War was fought between the British and French and the Qing Dynasty as imperialism reached its height between 1856 and 1860.	94
PLA	The People's Liberation Army.	58
PRC	The People's Republic of China.	130

General References

Bell, D. A. (2008) *China's New Confucianism*. Princeton, NJ: Princeton University Press.

Brown, K. (2008) *The Rise of the Dragon*. Witney, Oxon: Chandos Publishing.

Charter 08, a plea for human rights in China (complete text available from *AsiaNews.it* on www.asianews.it/index; accessed 17 June 2009).

Clegg, J. (2009) *China's Global Strategy: Towards a Multipolar World*. London/New York: Pluto Press.

Darwin, C. (1859) *On the Origin of Species*. London: John Murray.

Dawson, R. (ed.) (1964) *The Legacy of China*. Oxford: Oxford University Press.

Dewey, J. (1928) *Freedom in the Modern World* (ed. Horace M.Kallen). New York: Coward McCann.

Edwardes, M. (1961) *Asia in the European Age 1498–1955*. London: Thames & Hudson.

Financial Times (2009) *Regulatory Remits* in the Lex Column, US edn, May 21, p. 14.

Fukuyama, F. (1995) *Trust – The Social Virtues and the Creation of Prosperity*. London: Hamish Hamilton.

Haley, G. T. and Tan, C.-T. (1999) East vs West: Strategic Marketing Management Meets the Asian Networks. *Journal of Business and Industrial Marketing,* 14 (2), pp. 91–101.

Hutton, W. (2007) *The Writing on the Wall: China and the West in the 21st Century*. New York: Little, Brown.

Hume, D. (1739–40) *A Treatise of Human Nature*, Book I (available Oxford University Press).

Jacques, M. (2009) *When China Rules the World: The Rise of the Middle Kingdom and the End of the Western World*. London: Allen Lane.

Legge, J. (1893) *The Chinese Classics*. Oxford: Oxford University Press.

Lovell, J. (2007) *The Great Wall: China Against the World, 1000 BC–AD 2000*. New York: Grove Press.

Lunding, A. (2006) Global Champions in Waiting: Perspectives on China's Overseas Direct Investment. Available at: www.dbresearch.com; accessed May 10, 2009.

Mackinnon, A. and Powell, B. (2008) *China Calling: A foot in the global door.* Basingstoke: Palgrave Macmillan.

Orwell, G. (1986) *Burmese Days*. London: Random House.

Orwell, G. (1936) *Keep the Aspidistra Flying*. London: Victor Gollancz.

Pope, A. (1733–34) *Essay on Man*, Epistle II, lines 1–2 (Maynard Mack, available Routledge, London, 1982).

Pope, A. (1733–4) *Essay on Man*. Epistle III, lines 303–4 (Maynard Mack, available Routledge, London, 1982).

Smith, A. (1776) *The Wealth of Nations*, Vol. II (ed. Edwin Cannan) (available London, Methuen, 1950).

Smith, A. (1759) *The Theory of Moral Sentiments*. London: A. Millar.

Spence, J. D. (1993) *Chinese Roundabout*. New York/London: W. W. Norton.

Time (2009) *Buying Binge* by Bill Powel, March 5. Available at: www.time.com/time/magazine.

Wittgenstein, L. (1953) *Philosophical Investigations*. New York: Macmillan.

Xinran (2008) *China Witness: Voices from a Silent Generation*, trans. from Chinese by E. Tyldesley, N. Harman and J. Lovell. London: Chatto & Windus.